Through Fear To Faith

A Spiritual Journey

Thomas Cowan Starnes

Bloomington, IN      Milton Keynes, UK

AuthorHouse™
1663 Liberty Drive, Suite 200
Bloomington, IN 47403
www.authorhouse.com
Phone: 1-800-839-8640

AuthorHouse™ UK Ltd.
500 Avebury Boulevard
Central Milton Keynes, MK9 2BE
www.authorhouse.co.uk
Phone: 08001974150

© *2006 Thomas Cowan Starnes. All rights reserved.*

No part of this book may be reproduced, stored in a retrieval system, or transmitted by any means without the written permission of the author.

First published by AuthorHouse 9/28/2006

ISBN: 1-4259-6505-9 (sc)

Library of Congress Control Number: 2006908283

Printed in the United States of America
Bloomington, Indiana

This book is printed on acid-free paper.

For Wave,

Who, for all but eighteen of the years written about,

Has been by my side

Table of Contents

Acknowledgements...ix

Introduction...xiii

Tennessee Years..1

The Promised Land 12

A Child of the Church 28

Leaving Home..45

"Called" to Preach 57

Seminary Days – Questions Begin..68

"Comes the Moment to Decide" 81

Joining the People Called Methodist 100

"Born Again" in Therapy 115

"Born Again" Again in AA..142

What I Have Had to Say 163

What I Have Read..188

"Sing them Over Again to Me" 192

Living in Benton's Shadow 203

Running Out of Time 212

"Bring it on in, Reverend"..222

Acknowledgements

I am indebted to my sister Jane for filling me in on the Tennessee years – those long ago rough years most of which I missed, and all of which my brother Luther missed, save for a few months. I am further indebted to Jane for accepting, maybe reluctantly, the care of me when I came home from the hospital to begin making my way in this world. Mama made these care assignments, my older sisters tell me, whenever a new baby came along, and Jane made me my first rattle: a Calumet Baking Powder can containing a few pebbles.

I am also indebted to those others who lived under the same roof with me. Florine, the oldest child, who, like the rest of us sports a few psychic scars, yet, at eighty-seven, on most days, enjoys life and whose humor reminds me most of Mama. Ruth, child number five, my playground protector, and the one who introduced me to Eugene Field's, "Little Boy Blue", just passed the four score year mark having battled her way through cancer, and is making the most of living with the little bit of sight that macular degeneration hasn't destroyed. Luther, the last of mama's brood, who gets a fair amount of copy in the upcoming pages, simply because we have been buddies for a very long time, just got his biblically allotted three score and ten. Although the subject never comes up, it has to cross his mind because it crosses mine, which one of us will be left standing to say a few last words over the other one.

If Elizabeth had lived, child number two, she would be eighty-five, and, no doubt, still a member of the church that the rest of us chose to leave. She worried a lot about the state of our souls, but family ties held us together, and we were all with her when cancer took her away at fifty-five. Benton, child number four, would have been eighty-one, had muscular dystrophy not cut his life short at age twenty-seven. His life was such a gift to the family. And Lucille, child number six, my playmate and sparring partner, would be seventy-eight had not cancer gotten the last word just about this time ten years ago,

And, of course, there's Mama and Daddy – which is what we Tennesseans called our fathers and our mothers – to whom I am deeply indebted. There is little doubt that not a single one of the eight of us was a part of any parenting plan. But none of us ever felt unwanted. We were loved and cared for and nurtured in the faith.

Any list of people to whom I owe a lot would have to include those who have sat in all those pews out there in front of me for all those years. Some of them I mention in the pages to follow, but an awful lot I do not. There is a decided trade deficit between me and all these saints: they gave me more than I ever gave them.

Finally, there are those that now make up my family. Wave, to whom this book is dedicated and about whom I write a great deal, is the love of my life and who packed an over abundance of commitment into that simple "I do" she spoke in front of that Ohio church altar fifty-two years ago. Vicky, our eldest, who will reach the half century mark this year, has the scars that all new parents, of necessity I think, inflict on their first born. I had a "cracker" organist who said that first children were like first waffles – they needed to be thrown away. Vicky was a keeper, and her granddaddy Starnes would be so proud. She preaches, and lives, the faith that held him steady: God is faithful and will provide. Tommy, ever the middle child, never comfortable with conflict, settled on the law as a way for him, I suppose, to make a living working at reconciliation. His faith is a search, yet deep down, he, too, believes that this is his Father's world. And darling Floyd, the baby, who will be forty-six come October, never met a person he didn't like, simply because the gospel he heard growing up said that we ought to love everybody, regardless, and if there were more like him in this world there would never be another lie told and we would all find a way to just get along.

These three of ours have brought John, Barbara and Carlos into my life, and they in turn have blessed Wave and me with Keott, Rachel, Hannah, Jacob, Dylan, Joe and Danny. All those bumper stickers about the joys of grand parenting that always seemed a bit overblown, are now my sentiments, exactly. What a treasure these precious gifts from God are. And if Hannah's thirteen year old heart is really picking up intimations from above, one day she will join her Mama, her great uncle Luther, her second cousin Patricia, and her two granddaddies and find her own way to tell the "old, old story of Jesus and his love."

Introduction

This book got its start almost twenty years ago. A book, though, was the farthest thing from my mind when I sat at my desk that May Monday morning and began to write. All I knew was that I had to fashion some sort of response to a question one of Washington, D. C.'s more notable "talking heads" had asked on a local television news panel: "and just what is a Nazarene, anyway?"

The topic that Saturday night on "Agronsky and Company" was the presidential candidacy of Gary Hart. This was just days before Donna Rice became a household name, so Senator Hart was still a major player in the race for the Democratic nomination. Some non-sex character questions were already rumbling around: he had changed his name as well as his age, and had slightly altered the name of his college. It was this bit of past doctoring – making Bethany Nazarene College be, simply, Bethany College – that caused James J. Kilpatrick to ask the question that prompted me to put pen to paper.

I had heard of Gary Hart long before his name was in the news. He was one of us: us being a rather large group – spread out all over the country – of persons who had made the decision to leave the church that had nurtured them in the faith.

The church in question was the Church of the Nazarene, a relatively small – but fast growing – conservative denomination that was established in 1908 by a group of people – mostly Methodists – who felt that the then contemporary followers of John Wesley had strayed a bit from the teachings of their founder.

I had no idea of my audience that Monday morning; I just wrote. My opening line was a suspicion that it just could be I was the only guy in town (I was pastor at Capitol Hill Methodist Church at the time) who could understand why Gary Hart might not want to dwell on his religious past, because I, like him, was a "backslidden" (their word) Nazarene.

What followed was a mini spiritual journey centering on what it was like growing up in a restrictive religious environment, the pain of not being able to go to movies or school dances, and always feeling a bit out of it socially. I also wrote of the joy in finding a church that gives one room to grow.

This was pre-word processing days for me, so I gave my long hand scribbles to the church secretary to transcribe, and, when that was done, I had no idea what to do with them.

To this day, I find it hard to believe that I stuffed those words into an envelope addressed to the editor of the Washington Post. Aside from a sermon and an article or two, I had never had anything published. Who did I think I was just throwing something over the transom at the prestigious Post? If anyone there was assigned to open such unsolicited stuff, I had visions of Meg Greenfield and company splitting their sides over this small time Methodist preacher presuming to think that they had time for such pious drivel.

Then, while that missile was en route, the flash bulbs went off behind the shrubs in front of Gary Hart's Capitol Hill town house, and his presidential bid was toast. Not only was his candidacy out of the question, so also was any notion, however slight, I might have entertained that my piece would ever see the light of day. Or so I thought.

But Thursday, I got a call from the Post. They would like to run the article Sunday. Would I be around? They wanted to send a courier over with some suggested editing. I have cherished this next comment: "the suggested changes are minimal." Since I had not re-written anything, it surprised me to hear that.

The article ran on Sunday, and the calls started coming. Wire services picked it up, it appeared in papers all over the country, and it was selected for "The Best of the Post." It was pretty good writing, but not that good. What helped it along was Gary's fall from grace. One southern paper ran it next to a cartoon that showed Gary's pants down around his ankles, his boxer shorts had hearts on them, and a bimbo was clutching his ankles. They titled my piece, "What's in Gary's Hart."

Notoriety aside, my best guess is that what grabbed a fair number of people was that little snippet of my faith journey that had me moving out of, what was, for me anyway, a restrictive religious environment, so that I might find a faith that was my own. At least this is what most of the letters and calls indicated.

Since that time, high on my "to do" list has been the stretching of that article into a more fully fleshed out recounting of my faith journey. The public response to my article had something to do with this desire of mine to tell a bit more of my faith story. But other factors have been at work egging me on.

One is the reaction I used to get from my congregations when I would go public with some of my wrestling matches with God. Even before it became good homiletical form for preachers to stick pieces of their story into their sermons, I would do so, and invariably these were the sermons that elicited the most positive feedback.

Another factor working on me concerns the comments I get from those who, like me, left the church of our childhood, but who, unlike me, left the church altogether. And, to be honest, can't understand how on earth I have managed to live out my life "feeding at the trough of organized religion," as one of them has not so delicately put it. This is what one of my friends from those long ago years said in a recent e-mail.

"I would truly like to know about your journey from growing up as a Nazarene and then moving into the Methodist Church. How did you keep from just throwing it all out? I certainly struggled for years over religious beliefs after I left seminary, and while the morals remained, I finally just gave up on religion … . I do not mean to pry into your private life but if you ever get the urge to write about the transformation of your own beliefs, I would be very interested. I have simply contented myself by thinking, well, I am here, and do not do the things that would be destructive to myself and to others and if there is something out there after this life, then okay, but I do not believe that there is."

This book is for Herb and some of those others I sojourned with years ago who can't quite figure out why I am still, as we used to sing back then, "pressing on the upward way."

This book is also for me. Faith is a journey not a destination. We never really arrive. The best we can hope for is that dimmed view that Paul likened to peering through a darkened glass. Many of the questions that shoved me into a denomination that would give me room to roam remain unanswered. But I have kept at it – this seeking – and hoping against hope that the way will become clearer.

Perhaps this is best stated in my email response to Herb.

"You asked about how I have kept at it. I sometimes wonder. I have never been comfortable with the concept of 'call.' It is something I have from time to time questioned; spent a fair amount of time in therapy wondering about. But there has been something going on inside me that has kept me at it. Part of it, I think, has been my search for my own faith. Do you remember reading about John Wesley's struggle – how he felt that he didn't have the necessary faith to do what he was doing? He shared this with a Moravian named Peter Boehler who told him, 'Preach faith until you have it, and then because you have it you will preach it.' Maybe that is what I have been doing – trying to find my own way by preaching it out."

Maybe this is what I am doing now – still trying to find my own way, by writing it out.

Chapter 1

"We are all of us what we are to be by the time we are ten years old."
Soren Kierkegaard

Ancient wisdom says that the longest journey begins with the first step. The first step on my journey of faith was actually taken by my father. And he took it down the center aisle of the Cowan, Tennessee, Nazarene Church on a balmy summer night in 1936.

I think it was balmy, because an early memory of mine is being on a front porch swing with Ruth, one of my five older sisters, and listening to the singing coming through the open windows of the church across the street. My four year old ears couldn't make sense of the words being sung, which, I guess, is the reason that this hazy memory is of my sister and me coming up with a lyric of "he'll eat my bones." Perhaps ten-year-old Ruth was already doing what I would later do by singing such things as, "On a hill faraway stood an old Chevrolet."

My Dad, seated in that church across the street, had no trouble hearing clearly the words of at least one song that summer evening. Actually, the song that moved him out of his seat and down the center aisle of that church to "give his heart to the Lord" wasn't sung at all. Rather, the evangelist who had come to this little railroad town church to conduct its annual summer revival played it on a slide trombone.

"There were ninety and nine that safely lay in the shelter of the fold,

But one was out on the hills away, Far off from the gates of gold."

There was no question in my Dad's mind that night; he was that one lost sheep.

If you were to construct a time line for our family, it would not be stretching it to mark the years before 1936 as B.C. and those after as A.D. The "Before Christ" part does not mean that we were pagans. Not at all. We came from a long line of "church people." In my father's farm family, after the evening chores were completed and the supper dishes cleared, Papa Starnes would read from the family Bible and lead in prayer. Church continued to play a role in my father's life as he and Mama worked to establish their own family. During those family forming years my Dad sang in the choir and taught a Sunday school class in the local Cumberland Presbyterian Church, and all of us children were baptized.

But in the summer of 1936, the Starnes' family was in trouble. This was before "dysfunctional" was a word attached to families. My guess is that if the word were used at all in the Tennessee hill country, its reference point would be some piece of farm equipment. Given what we know now, it would not be a stretch to label our family as dysfunctional. My younger brother, Luther – child number eight – had been born in March. My father did have a steady job – not an insignificant accomplishment in those depression years – albeit a low paying apprenticeship. My mother's family was keeping us in food and clothing. We were moving from rental house to rental house. And more and more of the little bit my father was able to earn went to the local bootlegger.

Not only were we dysfunctional, we were an embarrassment to both the Cowan and the Starnes families. When Papa Cowan was told that Mama was pregnant with child number eight, he said, "My God, they haven't paid for the last one yet." Papa had signed a note for the hospital bill when I had been born four years earlier. He then said, "Are they running a race with Mary Doll Hornbuckle?" The Hornbuckles were "white trash" – a necessary designation, I suppose, since in those days, "trash" was usually reserved for blacks. We were an embarrassment to two well-respected, proud families. And we lived in a town named after our Cowan ancestors.

Troubled families were not at all uncommon during those depression years. My parents had married quite young – on the same day that Mama graduated from high school. Early marriage wasn't that uncommon then, and a fair number, like my father, didn't even wait to finish high school. But families like the Starneses and the Cowans had higher hopes for their children. My mother's family had planned for her to take a state test and be certified to teach school for a year, with the obligation to attend summer school and work toward a degree. It is unclear what my father's family had in mind for him.

Whatever plans the two families had for their children, notwithstanding, on May 18, 1917, Grady Duncan Starnes and Mary Lucille Cowan were married, and moved into a small farmhouse on some land that Papa Starnes had bought. Papa's plan was to build a larger house on this property and farm it. Which is what he did a few years later, forcing my father and mother to find another place to live, not only for the two of them, but also for Mary Florine and Elizabeth Duncan.

The father on the other side of the family became the port in this storm. Papa Cowan, an engineer on the Nashville, Chattanooga, and St. Louis Railroad, had recently bought his family's farm, and asked my Dad to farm it for him. However, just one year later, Mama's father sent the family packing, having decided to mix a bit of farming with his railroading. So, the five of them – Anna Jane having joined the mix – moved into one side of a rental house, and my dad – burying his pride – helped his father-in-law run the farm.

Since farming didn't pay very well, never mind the insecurity of it, and with his growing family, my Dad did what quite a few other southern men were doing, including his younger brother, James Rowe: he headed to Akron, Ohio to work in the rubber shops. Grady Benton, the first son, was born there.

The work in Akron was steady and my parents made new friends, but wanderlust struck again; this time of their own making. "Lucille was homesick," was my father's take on the reasons for the move. The fact that she was expecting child number five probably had something to do with her wanting to be near her extended family. So it was back to Tennessee and home.

My mother's family, however, wasn't all that welcoming. She had written, telling of their eminent return to Cowan – no doubt including the announcement of another Starnes baby on the way – and asking if they had a few extra rooms where our family might live until we got settled. Her family said no.

The Starnes side of the family did have some room, so after a couple months shy of two years in Ohio, Mama, Daddy and their four children returned to Tennessee, and moved in with Papa and Nannie Starnes, in the very same "big" house on the Starnes farm – the house where Daddy and Mama had lived for a brief period five years before. It was there sister Ruth was born.

None of my sisters remember where my father worked in those immediate post-Akron years. Their best guess is that he fell back to his agricultural dependency. They do remember that it was not long before he signed on as an apprentice machinist with the Cumberland Portland Cement Company in Cowan. He was working there when Lucille Cowan was born in May, 1928. It is a source of mild astonishment that even though the family moved a lot, they have no recollection of ever doing any packing. What they do remember, though, is Mama reminding them in the morning not to come back to that house after school, and if they didn't remember where the new house was, they should go by Nannie Cowan's; she would direct them.

Added to the family's economic insecurity was concern over Benton's health. It had become increasingly evident that something was not quite right about his walking. He had not walked as early as the other children and when he did start to take a few steps, his gait was strange and he fell a lot. Although, he started to school on schedule, he became easy prey for childhood cruelty, and even though his older sisters tried to defend him – chasing away the kids who would push him over – my parents thought it best to keep him at home.

Muscular dystrophy at that time was a mysterious disease. The doctors at first speculated that he might have had polio as a child. One of my mother's aunts took him to the Shriner's Hospital in St. Louis. Even there, as it turned out, notions about this disease bordered on the primitive: the doctors said that Benton had an hereditary muscle disease that would eventually cripple all of the children. And worse even than those prospects, no child with this disease had ever lived beyond the age of 21.

My sister Jane remembers the gloom that settled over the house. But, life went on, she said, and, true to form, Mama was pregnant again.

With me. As each birth came, those who knew wondered how long the odds would continue to go in Mama's favor. You see after she lost the first child – a still birth – the family doctor told my father that Lucille should not get pregnant again. He said her heart was enlarged, and another pregnancy might kill her.

It didn't, and I was born in June, 1932 – child number seven. Just months later the Depression shut the doors of the cement plant, and my father, hat in hand, asked Papa Starnes if he could move his wife and seven children into the little tenant house that Papa owned, and help him out on the farm. Papa said, "Grady, you can't live in there. It's not fit. Besides, I have potatoes stored there." My dad said, "Just say that I can and we'll clean it out." Papa relented, and Daddy and the girls bagged the potatoes and scrubbed the place out with Lysol. This was the house where I learned to crawl and took my first steps.

My father's wages were fifty cents a day, a cow for milk, chickens for eggs, and all the vegetables and fruit that could be eaten. Potatoes were eaten three times a day. School lunches of biscuits left over from breakfast, covered with butter and filled with fried potatoes – also left over from breakfast – were wrapped in newspaper. Sometimes a tomato or jelly was added to the biscuit.

In the winter, when there wasn't enough work to do on the farm, Daddy sold Watkins products door to door. He had done some of this before the move back to the farm when the cement plant closed. He had bought an Essex car. Actually, Papa Cowan bought it for him, by signing a note at the local bank. But the Essex sat in the yard because there wasn't enough money to buy license tags for it. Years before, my sister Jane had won the "prettiest baby" prize at the Franklin County Fair. Her three dollar prize was put in a savings account which tripled in value. My father asked Jane if he could buy a pig with it. His pitch to her was that they could raise piglets and make some much needed money. Jane relented and the pig did become an income producer. Reality tends to trump sentimentality, and the day came when the pig, pet though she was, was also put on the market, and it was this windfall that put tags on the Essex.

Another cloud was settling in over the Starnes household: my Dad's drinking was becoming a problem. Knowing what we know now about alcoholism, it is little wonder. Abuse of alcohol was scattered among my Dad's family. His grandfather, Joe Bibb Starnes traveled the countryside in a horse drawn wagon filled with needles, thread, flour, sugar and other household items. Tucked in among those staples was a jug of moonshine that Grandpa Starnes sipped from during the course of his daily rounds. Also in the wagon was a long plank that Grandma Starnes used to roll her husband out of the wagon at the end of the day, when the horse, Tom, knowing the route, would pull the wagon up to the front of the house.

In the fall of 1933, the Cement Plant re-opened and my father was called back to work. The family moved into a house in Decherd, Tennessee, next door to the Methodist Church parsonage. Daddy's drinking continued, and Mama started going out with him at night, her stated reason being that she wanted to keep an eye on him. Her keeping an eye on him made the neighbor's question who was keeping an eye on her seven children. Florine, the oldest at fourteen, had that responsibility. An otherwise happy, contented eighty-five year old, still bears the scars of constantly watching to see when her Mama and Daddy would come home; wondering even if they would.

Being next to the Methodist parsonage was fortuitous. Since there was no Cumberland Presbyterian Church in Decherd, the family began attending the Methodist Church, and it was to the Methodist preacher living next door that my Dad gave the first indication that he needed help: he confessed that he really wanted to get his life in order.

The family moved back to Cowan after about a year. My sisters don't remember the stated reasons for all these moves. I have asked if we were deadbeats and skipped out on rent payments. They say they don't think that was it. Their explanation is that few folks – outside of farmers – owned their homes; most people rented. And when a better house came along, they would just move.

Remember the Essex car. Working as an apprentice and supporting a family of nine, not to mention keeping yourself in bootleg whiskey, left no money to pay off the note that Papa Cowan had signed to enable my Dad to buy the car. Mama's brother, Robert, was still living at home and wanted a car. Papa told him to go over to our house and get the Essex. When my father got home from work, Mama told him that Papa had taken it back for the money still owed on it.

As my Dad's drinking increased, his sense of responsibility lessened. One Friday after work he was standing on the street corner with some buddies when a Greyhound bus arrived. One of them said, "Let's go to Chattanooga, Grady," and they did. Taking with them the paycheck my Dad had just picked up. Daddy came home on Sunday night, full of remorse. He hadn't just spent the weekend in Chattanooga; he had also spent his whole paycheck. Again, mama's family came to the rescue with food that would last until the next Friday.

Mama would cry and fuss after each of these binges, Florine remembers, and she, the surrogate mother, would tell Mama to be nice or Daddy might leave. Jane, ever the one to straight talk Daddy – actually, the only one in the family to do so – would tell him that he ought to be ashamed of himself.

Filled with remorse, he would try. But once you reach a certain point alcohol takes control. In a visit a couple years back with my mother's sister, Avaline, I asked her about those days. I especially wanted to know a bit more about those first four years of my life when my Dad's drinking was spinning out of control. A marvelous story teller with a wonderful sense of humor, even at ninety-four, Aunt Avaline told me of the time that Nannie Cowan asked Daddy to drop by and take a look at her sewing machine. It wasn't working properly. The sewing machine was where Nannie kept a small bottle of whiskey, which she delicately referred to as her cough medicine. Daddy did stop by and fixed the sewing machine. After he had gone, Aunt Avaline said, Nannie came out of the sewing room, empty bottle in hand, and said, "That son-of-a-bitch Grady drank my cough medicine."

That was a Daddy drinking story I had never heard. Others I had heard. Like the time he was out with some of his drinking buddies and their car, with my father driving, got too close to the edge on a mountain road and tumbled to the bottom – rolling over and over – landing on a rock with its four wheels spinning. I was also told about the time my Dad and one of his friends sat me down between them on a motorcycle seat and off we went speeding through the streets of Cowan.

A couple years ago my son, Floyd, thought it would be nice to get some of these Starnes family stories recorded, so he brought his camcorder along to our family Christmas get together. After the meal and gift exchange, Floyd sat the five of us remaining children down and told us to talk.

We had been going for about ten minutes – sharing our versions of the stories we all knew – when Florine, the oldest, started to talk and then stopped. She said she didn't think she could continue. Florine is the shyest of the bunch – given to sitting back and letting the rest of us rattle on – so we kept urging her to go ahead and continue, not understanding that it was the delicate nature of what she was trying to say that was causing her hesitancy and not her natural shyness.

Her story, that she finally found courage enough to share, concerned the days immediately following Luther's birth. The eighth and last child, Luther was born at home as were most of us, except Lucille and me. It was an uneventful birth, proving, among other things, that Mama's heart was stronger than the doctors thought. He was a big, pretty baby, and Mama was doing fine, so my Dad, feeling this was a cause for celebration, took off with one of his buddies and stayed out all night.

The next day, given the balmy March weather, the windows were open, and Florine, as she told us, was upstairs, and outside, just beneath the window in her room, she heard Daddy say to the buddy he had spent the night with, "Wasn't that the best piece of cock meat last night you ever saw." For almost seventy years, she had carried that story around with her – never telling it to anyone.

That was the Starnes family as the summer of 1936 arrived. We were the talk of the town – in a less than flattering way – and an embarrassment to two respectable families. As well as an embarrassment to ourselves – at least to those of us who were old enough to understand all that was happening – and most certainly to my father. He had, at one time, been offered a position in a bank. His younger brother was doing well. And here he was, in a low paying apprenticeship, drinking up most of the little he made, moving from house to house, cheating on his wife, and watching as her family put food on his table.

But all this was about to change. Across the street from where we were living was a Nazarene Church. My sister Jane used to go there with her best friend. What impressed Jane, she says, was the loud music. Like most small towns, there were few secrets, and when Mama heard that Jane had been seen at that Holy Roller Church, she expressed her displeasure and suggested that Jane not go there anymore; these were not our kind of people.

However, Mama did not stand in the Nazarene Church doorway forbidding my Dad to enter, when, at the invitation of a neighbor, he went to one of the Nazarene Church's summer revival services. Any port in a storm I guess she thought. And it was that night, as he later came to sing, he "saw the light and the burden of his heart rolled away."

My father came home from that service, a changed person. It wasn't all that evident at the time. He had made many promises before. But there was hope among the family that this time around things would be different. When Papa Cowan – who had little time for those "holy rollers" – heard that Daddy had "got religion last night at the Nazarene Church," he said, "I don't care if he joins the Catholic Church (quite an admission to make in those anti-Catholic days) if he straightens out."

And that is precisely what happened. He never drank again. He became as we say, "a faithful member of Christ's holy church," and lived the twenty-two years he had left of life as a devoted and caring husband and father. And he gave me the first plank in my faith platform, which is: a person can change. Or, to put it in the words of the scriptures I was taught: "Old things can pass away and all things can become new."

This is why I could never toss it all aside – this faith of my father. I needed to leave the church he so dearly loved – the church that had been a lifesaver for him. I had to find a faith community that was less restrictive – one that made room for doubts and questions – and did not spend most of its time concerned with what I perceived to be rather picayune issues of right and wrong. What I have never been able to let go of, though, nor have I ever wanted to, really, is that church's belief that we, each of us, can change; or, as they put it, be born again.

Chapter 2

"All I have needed thy hand hath provided, great is Thy faithfulness…"
Thomas O. Chisolm

Robert A. Johnson in his memoir, <u>Balancing Heaven and Earth</u>, calls those chance happenings in his life – being in the right place at the right time, meeting a certain person – that occurred at the most opportune times, "slender threads." For my father, these "slender threads" were sure signs of God at work in his life. And they started to appear shortly after – in his words – "he gave his heart to the Lord" at that 1936 summer's revival meeting at the little Nazarene Church across the street.

The first of these slender threads came by way of the neighbor who had invited my father to go with him to the revival meeting. His son worked for the DuPont Company in Richmond, Virginia, and on one of his visits home to Tennessee, the son brought along a notice stating that machinists were needed at DuPont's operation in Wilmington, Delaware, and an application. My father filled out the application and sent it on its way. I have an early memory of all of us gathered around a dining room table trying to find tiny little Delaware on an atlas map. My sisters were all old enough to remember both the excitement and the dread of moving so far away – a distance that was rounded out to be a thousand miles. The response from DuPont was not long in coming: if the required interview went well, my Dad had the job.

The fall had always been a time for my anxieties to kick in, causing me to wonder, ever and again, if it had something to do with seeing my father take off to a strange place – a thousand miles away – in the October of my fourth year. I am sure that during those tumultuous early years of my life, at some level of awareness, Florine's fear of Daddy leaving and not coming back must have been my fear as well. The plan was that he would go on ahead for the interview, and, if hired, would find a place for us to live. His promise was that we would all be together for Christmas.

He got the job – a job that paid more than he had ever hoped to make. What he had, more than money, though, was a sense that he was beginning a new life. Finally, he had left home. No longer dependent on either set of parents; no longer near his old drinking buddies; his was a new day.

With a supportive community – a supportive faith community. One member of the Cowan Nazarene Church, Miss Daisy Sargent, worried about Daddy being alone in that northern city. What with his being, as the apostle Paul put it, a "babe in Christ," she was concerned that he just might slip back into his old ways. So she asked her pastor to get in touch with the Nazarene pastor in Wilmington, and within days of my father's arrival in Delaware, Brother Boggs (which is what we called our pastors then) knocked on the door of his boarding house room and invited him to church – another of those "slender threads."

After his conversion my father became an inveterate "testifier." Part of the ritual in the Nazarene Church was for persons to "testify" or publicly witness to their faith. Daddy was so profoundly grateful for God's grace that had worked this miracle in his life that he wanted to share his story with anyone he met. A co-worker was so moved by the account of his "born again" experience, and so convinced of both his sincerity and his integrity, that he offered my father his house for a few months. He and his wife were going to Florida for the winter and we were welcome to live there for the short time they would be away.

Not everyone would be together for Christmas, though. Florine would remain in Tennessee to graduate from high school in June, and Jane, finishing the eighth grade as valedictorian, would also stay behind to receive her honor. The decision to let Elizabeth not make the trip north had little or nothing to do with school. Named after Mama's mother, Elizabeth was always a favorite of the Cowans. Sis, as they called her, enjoyed special privileges. She stayed with Papa and Nannie Cowan a lot. During the lean years – which meant most, if not all, the time – she got new dresses and dolls, much to the dismay of her other sisters. One of Daddy's drinking stories centered around the Mother's Day when he rode by the Cowan house on a motorcycle, and seeing Nannie out on the lawn, shouted to her, "Miz Cowan, since it's mother's day, I'm gonna give you Sis." Nannie shouted back, "Git on out of here you crazy fool."

I marvel at the courage it took for my mother to board that train with five children in tow – one of whom was barely able to walk, and another just eight months old -- and make that long trip north to Delaware. Tennessee was home. That's where her supportive community was. It was her family, after all, that had helped us keep body and soul together. It must have occurred to her that this just might be another of Grady's fanciful notions – like the move to Akron had been; that there was a "promised land" out there somewhere, if only he could locate it. However, firmly committed to the promise she had made almost twenty years before, to stick it out for better or for worse, she put her fears and doubts aside, sold what little furniture we had – receiving just enough to cover the train fares – and left to join her husband in this new life of theirs.

I have no conscious memories either of our send off from Tennessee or the trip itself. What I have associated with that exodus of ours is a single visual image of sitting on a long seat – like those at the back of a bus – snuggled up closely to the persons on either side of me, whose faces I cannot make out, and a sound and a smell. The sound, for obvious reasons, is a train whistle, and the smell, for not so obvious reasons, is of bananas. Thirty-nine Novembers later, Mama's "bad heart" finally gave out. She had outlived Daddy and had stayed around long enough to see Benton through to the end of his life. The family was at Jane's house doing what families do after memorial services – eat and reminisce. I don't remember the conversation leading up to my saying that the smell of bananas and the sound of a train whistle arouse such comforting feelings in me. My sister Florine – the quiet one – then told us a story I, at least, had never heard.

On that November day in 1936, she, Elizabeth and Jane had come down to the Cowan depot to wish us well on our trip north. Grandpa Brakefield came, too. He was my mother's maternal grandfather. Tall, always dressed in black, a conductor on the Nashville, Chattanooga and St. Louis Railroad, he rarely spoke, no doubt the result of his deafness. He was an avid reader of the Bible as well as an equally avid quoter of scripture – quoting he did on little slips of paper that he left here and there around town, even going so far as to post them on telephone poles. Florine said that while we were all standing there waiting for the train, Grandpa Brakefield drove up in his Model A Ford Coupe, handed

Mama a grocery bag filled with bananas and snacks for the trip, then got back in his car and drove away not having said a single word. In the bottom of the bag – down under the bananas, apples, crackers and cheese – was a little slip of paper. On the paper were these words from Psalm 37: "I have been young, and now am old; yet have I not seen the righteous forsaken nor his seed begging bread."

Did my four-year-old head, or heart, sense the comfort those ancient words gave to this not yet forty-year old mother heading off to God knows where? Do you suppose she really believed the words her grandfather had given her – God's words, or so he believed – that all she would need would be provided? I am not sure. All I know is that the smell of bananas and the sound of a train whistle are comfort foods for my soul, and for want of a better explanation, I trace them back to Grandpa Brakefield's going away gift to us – a bag of fruit and the Psalmist's blessed assurance that all would be well.

That might not have been Mama's faith as we made our way north, but there is little doubt that it was the faith of my father. God was in all of this, he sincerely believed, leading him along, each step of the way. And who could doubt it. These "slender threads" just kept appearing. When time came for the owners of the house we moved into to return from Florida, a family at church suggested that we might move into the rental house they were leaving. For health reasons they were downsizing, and, for a reasonable price, we could have all of their furniture. Mama and Daddy were thrilled. The house was large enough to accommodate all of us, including the three girls who would be coming after school closed, and it was more and better furniture than we had ever had.

Believing that God was in it did not mean that all would go as planned. What it meant for my father was that even when things didn't go quite as expected or hoped for even, God was still present. And the first real

Through Fear to Faith

test of this new found faith of his came just when everything seemed to be going well. All the family was together, in a well-furnished house. For the first time in his life, he had a steady job with a reputable company. His employment future looked bright. The depression seemed to be on its last legs, thanks to his Democratic savior, FDR. It was then the notice came that he was "laid off."

My sisters tell me that they remember no panic on my Dad's part. By his own admission, not once during the rest of his life was he ever tempted to crawl back into the bottle. So, we can assume drowning his sorrow over losing a job never entered his mind as an option. My sister Jane (the family member with the best memory) recalls Daddy "testifying" that God brought him to Delaware and God would provide.

Which is what happened. Benton never walked again after the train trip. Papa Cowan arranged for a wheelchair to be ready for us when we changed trains in Chattanooga, and also for one to be available when we got to Wilmington. Delaware schools provided a home tutor for Benton. Miss Nickum taught him leatherwork and ceramic painting. Through a private agency, she arranged for him to get a wheelchair. She brought my sisters some of the most expensive re-sale designer clothes they ever had. She also talked my father into accepting funds she could get for him – funds that would pay him his regular salary while he was out of work. She convinced him that this was not welfare; it was merely using monies given by the more well to do, set aside to help those who were experiencing financial difficulties. This "living on the dole" was short-lived. Belanca Aircraft hired my father, and after just a few months there, Du Pont called him back, and he worked for them for the rest of his life. This is the way it went for him and for us. One door would close, and another would open. God would make a way.

Delaware was now home for us. We moved to a larger house in a better section of town – further away from downtown Wilmington. It had a front porch, a small yard, and larger rooms than the row house on Monroe Street. By giving his "testimony" to them – about Jesus having "saved him from sin" – my father convinced the Jewish owners of the Ogden and Howard furniture store to let him buy the furniture that the larger house required by paying a little bit each week.

The local Church of the Nazarene became our home away from home. Brother Boggs, who had first knocked on Daddy's rooming house door, met us at the train, and guided us through those early days of adjusting to new and strange surroundings. It was Brother Boggs, who delighted in calling me "Doubting Thomas," and those who know me well would credit him with a bit of prescience. The church had an active youth group – with enough boys in it to delight my sisters – especially Florine – who ended up marrying one of them, Irving Chappelle. Brother Jones, who succeeded Brother Boggs as pastor, started a church radio program. I have a picture taken in the broadcast studio. The choir is there with all of us Starnes children in it. Luther and I are sitting in the front row with my feet not quite touching the floor, and Luther's sticking straight out in front of him. Mama, the choir director, is standing in front, poised as though she is conducting, and right next to her, at the mike, is Brother Jones.

Delaware did appear to be the Promised Land my Father had envisioned. From his vantage point it was a land overflowing with its version of the biblical "milk and honey:" a comfortable place to live, good food, steady job, a loving family, and a house of worship where one could sing the praises of this gracious God who had caused all this to happen.

Wilmington, Delaware was, little by little, becoming home for the Starnes family. There were parks, a zoo, nearby restaurants where my older sisters could work, and public transportation. Although Mama still missed Tennessee, even she was content to finally be living a settled life in a pleasant community. The day came, however, when we would say goodbye to Wilmington, as we had said good-bye to Tennessee; not to travel a thousand miles, but a hundred, to our new home, in southern Delaware.

Since my father believed implicitly that God was leading him, he lived with one ear to the spiritual ground. Which is why he took seriously the announcement that DuPont was building a nylon plant in southern Delaware, and, if he wanted to, he could be transferred there. There were three reasons for his saying yes to the transfer. He had lost his job once in Wilmington, and when rehired, he was transferred from DuPont's machine shop to its Experimental Station. It sounded to him like there would be more job security at the new nylon plant in southern Delaware. In the second place, the southern end of the state was more rural, and farming was still in my Dad's blood. If he could not be a full-scale farmer, at least he could engage in some pretty serious gardening. The third reason for my Dad saying yes to the new job offer was his belief that opportunities like this didn't just happen. No. It was another instance of God guiding and directing his life.

So, on New Years' Day, 1940, the Wilmington Nazarene Church, along with the DuPont Company, moved us to our new home in Laurel, Delaware. DuPont provided the van that held our possessions, and Brother Jones, along with a couple from the church, loaded our family into their two cars. We moved into a farmhouse, and two years later moved into another house that was nearer town. Then, in 1944, my father was able to purchase his first house.

This is the house that shows up in my dreams. It was, and still is, the largest house in a little sailing village, with the biblical name, Bethel.

Sitting on an acre of land that ran all the way down to Broad Creek, this "mansion" (to us) not only meant that there would only be two of us children to a room, but there would be ground enough for a garden, and a shed that could function as a barn for our horse. Once again, according to my father, God had come through.

And so it went for the rest of his days. All he ever needed, God's hand provided. That was the faith that sustained him. No, everything didn't go as he hoped it would. He had his days of having to travel through deep and troubled waters. But never did he lose the assurance that, through it all, God was with him. He was not alone.

In the summer of 1956, my father bought a new top of the line Chevrolet for his and Mama's annual trip back to Tennessee. While there, he experienced what he referred to as "lights" in his eyes. He was examined and told to check in with his family doctor when he returned home. Which he did, and the test results were negative. In October he had the annual physical that DuPont required of all its employees. Those tests showed that his kidneys were not functioning properly. Further tests indicated that he was suffering from nephritis. He tried to keep working, but repeated hospitalizations forced his retirement in May 1957.

These were pre-dialysis days – those days coming in 1959. When my father would check into the hospital because fluid was collecting in his body, the treatment was primitive. Doctors would puncture his back and let the fluids drain into a receptacle. Daddy said he felt like a maple tree being tapped. This is the way his last years were spent: in and out of the hospital, gradually growing weaker.

When Mama died in 1975, my sister Jane found among the papers she had saved, a diary that my father had kept during those last few years. A lot of the entries are merely noting who came to see him, how much he weighed, and what Dr. Moyer told him when he made his rounds.

But some of the entries are "testimonies" to the goodness of God. He thanks God for his family – especially his boys. (A fact I wish Mama had told me. It could have cut a few hours off my therapy.) Then there is this one:

"October 15: Rest was not too good Sunday nite. Unrest or uneasiness in chest. Dr. Moyer came and discussed my coronary condition with me. Wgt. 193 pounds. I read 138th Psalm and marked portion. Gave me new hope and courage I need so much. I told a very interested nurse and a new roommate what the Lord had done for me in saving me. Had a quiet day. The Lord undertook for me wonderfully. The comforter came."

"Undertook" was the Nazarene's way of saying that God was faithful and would give you all you needed. The "comforter" to them was the Holy Spirit, who would be there in times of trouble to assure you that all would be well. And it was well for my Dad, right through to the end.

An end that almost seems scripted. He couldn't get well. His kidneys no longer functioned. The breakthrough in kidney treatment was a year away, and his heart was slowly giving out. Nobody talked about death – this was also pre-hospice days – especially doctors. But, at some level, we must have sensed that the end was near.

I had been the minister of a small Methodist Church during my seminary days, and had written my father telling him that given my serious doubts about the Nazarene Church's principle doctrinal tenet, I wasn't sure I could, with integrity, be a Nazarene pastor. His counsel to me was that since the church had educated me, maybe I ought to give it a try – at least for a year. I took his advice, and asked for a church near by. The closest one was just an hour's drive away.

Wave, Vicky, Tommy and I moved to the eastern shore in June of 1958, and we spent much of that summer traveling back and forth to visit him. The last time I saw him was the night before he died. I had spent the week counseling at our church's summer camp, and stopped off at the hospital on my way home. Mama had given him a new electric shaver, and he asked if I would shave him. I did half his face and told him I was going to leave it that way. I didn't. I also took a couple flowers from the vase on his table and stuck one in each of the two holes at the end of his hospital bed, and left them there. Kidding had, by then, become one of my weapons of choice against anxiety. I kissed him goodbye – he being the kissing parent – and left. I don't remember telling him that I loved him.

With Benton having died in 1952, the only other of his "boys," Luther, graduated from college and got married that summer of 1958. Daddy could not go with Mama to Massachusetts for the graduation. He was able to attend the wedding. The last picture we have of him is that typical wedding shot of both sets of parents acting as bookends to the bride and groom. My father looks as if he is being swallowed up by his tuxedo.

The other wonderful thing about that picture is that it is the only one we have of the altar and chancel of the church my Dad built. In 1950, as I was leaving for college, my father had a disagreement with the pastor of the Laurel Nazarene Church. Over the years, the southern end of Delaware, especially the town of Laurel, was not a garden spot for Nazarene Churches. Most everybody, who was anybody, belonged to either Centenary Methodist or St. Philip's Episcopal Church. The Laurel Nazarene Church, sociologically speaking, was on the other side of the tracks. Our little out of the way church didn't always get the choicest of preachers. They were all nice enough – some of them wonderful examples of the faith they attempted to preach – but, more often than not, lacking in business smarts. Which is why my father, for all practical purposes, had grown accustomed to running the church. He usually occupied one or more of the power positions most of the time. He used his good name to sign for church loans at the local bank. He did take certain privileges, like unscrewing "our pew" from the floor, inserting two doorstops under the front of both ends, screwing it back to the floor, thus creating the only reclining church pew I have ever seen. Most of the laity and most of the pastors appreciated all the work my father did for the church. His financial contributions – his tithe to the Lord as he referred to it – made him the highest contributor. On Sunday mornings, his car was turned into a church bus as he made the rounds picking up children whose parents either couldn't, or wouldn't, bring them to church and Sunday school. My father was the undisputed lay leader of the Laurel Nazarene Church.

Then Brother Taylor came to town. Educated, and with a touch of class, it was soon obvious that he was a cut or two above those who had preceded him as pastor of that southern Delaware Church. He and Daddy got along rather well. They joined in finishing up some of the work on the new parsonage that had been built for the previous minister, and successfully completing a major building addition to the church: an extension of the chancel, and the construction of a bell tower.

It was during this construction that Brother Taylor and my father parted company. The details of it all escape me; perhaps I never knew all the details. My guess is that it had a lot to do with my Dad's assumed position as presumptive leader of the church. By default he had been that: floating loans, making decisions, unscrewing pews, with little challenge from anyone. I can only assume that Brother Taylor let him know, maybe in subtle ways, that he was the appointed chief shepherd of this flock, and he intended to fill this post.

There could have been something else at work here. Not too far from Laurel was a little wooden frame building that housed a struggling congregation of about twenty or thirty people. My parents decided to go there and help them out. This didn't affect me a great deal. I personally liked Brother Taylor. He was the first one who ever said to me, "Thomas, do you think God is calling you to preach." The youth group in Laurel was a large group – containing many of my friends. But I was getting ready to leave home for college.

Not so with Luther and my sisters. The sisters were all married now, but when it came to the church of choice, Daddy's choice seemed always to prevail. So the whole family left Laurel Nazarene Church and joined the church in the neighboring town of Seaford.

It grew a bit at a time. But my father had this itch to build a church. What was needed was a preacher who, one, would be willing to come to such a hopeless situation, and two, knew something about building churches. One such minister did come, and he, along with my Dad, purchased a choice lot in a new housing development along a prominent street. The two of them found an Episcopal Church in a small town near the shore that became the model.

The last year that my Dad worked – already suffering from the disease that would kill him – he would leave work and go by the church site to help with the construction. Quite often Mama would bring him supper, and he would work on into the evening. In the Nazarene Church, it was the rule, not the exception, that the pastor would be the construction manager. Without paying an architect or a contractor and using a lot of donated labor, congregations could build new buildings at minimal cost. Working in the time between hospital stays, Daddy got to see his church built. He also got to see his baby boy married there. The church is a real estate office now. Although the steeple has been removed, it still looks like a church. At least it looks that way to me.

I used the word scripted about my father's death. Not only had I come home, and Luther had graduated from college and been married in Daddy's new church, but his youngest sister and her daughter had come from Tennessee to see him. Not many of the Tennessee relatives had made this trip over the years. Papa Starnes came once to announce his intention to marry the woman who owned the farm adjacent to his, but he lost his nerve and made the announcement in a letter he wrote after his return home. The only other member of my father's family that had come to Delaware was his brother.

Seeing Aunt Mary Lou and Emma Jean was such joy for my father. He held court in his hospital room, and ordered a trip to the ocean for his landlubbing Tennessee kinfolk the next day. On our annual summer vacation trips to Tennessee my favorite place to stay was Aunt Mary Lou and Uncle W.T.'s house. And my favorite cousins were their children, Frank and Emma Jean. So I invited myself along for that Saturday morning trip to the beach.

The only memory I have of that Saturday is our pulling into the driveway, and my sister Elizabeth meeting us at the door telling us that Daddy had just died. In a recent visit in Tennessee with Emma Jean, she told me that Aunt Mary Lou always worried that their trip to see Daddy had been too much excitement for him. I assured Emma Jean that by the time of their visit, his heart had been so weakened by nephritis that his days were numbered. And far from doing him harm, their visit allowed him to connect one last time with the family he loved and the land that in his heart he had never left.

Daddy's was the first funeral in the church he had built. His coffin rested in the place where he had stood with Mama two months before when their baby had been married. Somewhere along the way Daddy said he wanted "Going Home" played at his funeral. This request no doubt had something to do with this being the music that was played as Franklin Roosevelt's body was brought north from Warm Springs, Georgia. I am also sure it had not a little bit to do with my Dad's faith that when his time came, he would be going home. One of his favorite hymns, along with "There Were Ninety and Nine," was "A Child of the King." Whenever this hymn would be sung in church, my Dad's eyes would get filled with tears; especially so when we would get to the last verse.

> "A tent or a cottage, why should I care,
>
> They're building a palace for me over there.
>
> Though exiled from home, yet still I may sing,
>
> All glory to God, I'm a child of a king."

No wonder he would shed tears of joy. Who would have thought it? All those years when he just couldn't seem to find his place in life, living in his version of "tents and cottages," and now, thanks to a loving and gracious God, his life had purpose and meaning. Not only that, he also had the assurance that this same God would supply all his needs and would, one day, welcome him home.

The "welcoming home" part of my Dad's faith I will get to in a later section. Right now my concern is the "supplying all his needs" part. And of that I am sure. I saw it happening.

Which is why in leaving my Dad's church, I never strayed very far from his faith – this faith of his in the faithfulness of God. My daughter says I was forever telling her that "things have a way of working out." It's not something I remember putting in those exact words, but it is something

I have come to believe. Simply because that is the way my life has played out. "Slender threads" have woven themselves together in my experiences. Everything has not gone as I might have wished it to go. My life has not been without its struggles. There were times when I was skirting pretty close to the edge. I could have thought of this as the luck of the draw. But given my spiritual roots, I have chosen to believe, as my Dad chose to believe, that this was God at work in my life, fulfilling his promise that I would get all I would need and things would indeed work themselves out. Or as I love to sing:

> "Great is thy faithfulness, O God my Father,
>
> There is no shadow of turning with thee.
>
> All I have needed, thy hand has provided,
>
> Great is thy faithfulness, Lord unto me."

Chapter 3

"For where two or three are gathered in my name there am I in the midst of them."
                              Matthew 20:18

Some of my friends from those long ago years, like Herb, who have chucked this whole faith bit, is not just that I am a preacher, but that I still make a place in my life for the institutional church. The best answer I can give is to borrow a phrase I heard years ago, "child of the church." I have no idea whose phrase this is or even where I first heard it. Nor, for that matter, what it means. I know what it means to me, though: someone who has never known anything else but being a part of a church going family.

Even before my father's born again experience when I was four years old, church played a role in our family's life. Besides singing in the choir, Daddy taught a Bible class in the Cowan Cumberland Presbyterian Church. There were those occasional Sunday mornings when Mama would drop a raw egg in his coffee to help him deal with the ravages of the night before. It is fair to say, however, that the church did not occupy center stage position in my family until the years after that summer night revival in 1936.

What puzzles me is that my memories of church in those early Delaware years are scant at best. We went – a lot – but I have no memory of singing in that WDEL radio station, although I have the picture saying that I did. I have also been told that my brother Luther and I made our debut as church singers in that radio studio. You would think I would remember that, but I don't.

I have only three church memories of those Wilmington years. One is the picture in my mind of the sanctuary. It is your typically plain low protestant church with a center pulpit. Through the windows on the left side of the church I can see the chain linked fenced yard. Another memory is going into a room full of people who are talking in hushed tones and eating. This was a gathering in the home of a church family whose little girl had been burned to death when the gas oven flamed and ignited her dress. My third memory is the party the church gave me when I was going to have my tonsils removed. The only present I remember receiving was a coloring book and a box of colors; a present I kept even though a cold cancelled the removal of the tonsils I still have.

What I find strange about this near blank I draw when it comes to church life is that I have so many other memories of those early Delaware years. The sight of a toy sailboat will bring to mind those carefree days of playing in Tenth Street Park. I read of a Catholic priest who has died, and I will, on occasion, remember the time my sister Ruth took me to the neighborhood Roman Catholic Church to get in line with other mourners and view their beloved priest lying in repose. That memory could have seared itself into my brain because it was my first encounter with holy water, and while trying to figure out what I was to do with it after having dipped my hand into the bowl, like the woman in front of me had, I proceeded to stumble into her – not noticing that she had stopped long enough to kneel and make the sign of the cross. Passing a street vendor selling half smokes on a busy downtown Washington, D.C. street corner, the aroma will take me all the way back to those Saturday mornings when I would walk downtown with my father and we would eat one of those delicacies that no ball park hotdog – or any hot dog for that matter – has ever come close to duplicating. Standing in a Subway sandwich shop – staring at the collection of cold cuts – my heart will sometimes bring to mind those early submarine sandwich days, when "hoagies" were the Friday night treat in the Starnes house. Daddy would bring some home with him after work, and they would be our supper as we listened to Joe Louis fight. I remember sitting on the front steps of the Monroe Street house on hot summer nights, talking with our neighbors, and fending off mosquitoes with oil of citronella and burning cattails that had been brought from nearby marshlands. And just the other day, I told someone that the only American president I had ever seen was Franklin Roosevelt. It was on one of those hot dog Saturday mornings, that my father took me down to the corner of Monroe and 4th Street and we waved at FDR as he drove by in the back of a convertible.

The move to southern Delaware when I was seven marks the beginning of my conscious memories of church life. Why this is so – why I don't remember the Wilmington church years – I don't know. Since beginning this backward look at my faith journey, I have wondered if it might have had something to do with my becoming increasingly aware that belonging to an off brand denomination set one apart. I don't know enough about stages of early childhood development to conclude that being seven makes one more self conscious about things in their life that might mark them as different. All I can do is guess that coming into a school in the middle of the second grade, not seeing anyone who went to my church, hearing classmates talk about going to movies – a mortal sin for Nazarenes – and carnivals – equally taboo – and Sunday comics – heaven forbid – I must have begun to sense that there was a down side to this church life about which my father spoke so glowingly.

What I do know for sure is that little Tommy Starnes was born with the desire to please gene. I so wanted to belong and to be liked. One of my few memories of first grade is announcing to the class that my family had at one time had a pet bear. I think this boastful claim came on the heels of the teacher having read us a bear story. After I made this rather startling boast, she asked a probing question or two. Like, "where did you keep it, Tommy?" "In the back yard," I answered. "We had a metal fence," I tried to explain. Sensing I might be crushed by a total rejection of this tale about my imaginary pet, she indulged me with another question. "Where is the bear now, Tommy?" "We gave it to the zoo," was my answer. Where that story went from there, I don't remember.

Lost toward the end of a string of eight children, sandwiched between an older, crippled brother, who claimed most of Mama's attention, and a younger brother who had long curls until he was three (strands of which I found in Daddy's Bible that Mama had kept, and I was given after she died), the darling of everyone's eyes, I had to fight to make a place for myself.

And fight I did. The more my church stressed that we "were a peculiar people, zealous of good works" (somewhere in one of Paul's writings, I think), the more determined I became to not be set apart – especially in school. Profanity was one of my first attempts at joining the elementary school mainstream. On the playground during recess, at the slightest provocation, I would let loose a string of some of those forbidden words. Being as young as I was, I am certain my swearing skills left much to be desired, and I must have sounded like Mark Twain's wife who attempted to cure him of his swearing by trying to swear herself, only to have Twain tell her that she had the lyrics down but the melody was all wrong.

My profanity rebellion stage was short-lived. Perhaps I noticed that other elementary children weren't running around the playground shouting obscenities. However, my desire to be like everyone else didn't go away. So I learned to shade the truth a bit. When asked if I were going to the movies on Saturday, I never just said no. That would have been simple and easy and no one would have thought anything about it. But because I was convinced of my "outside looking in" position, I would make up some story about my not liking that particular actor. Later on in high school, when asked if I were going to the prom, it wasn't enough for me to say no, or maybe. I had to manufacture some kind of an excuse why I wouldn't be able to attend.

What I didn't know until years later was that where I went to church made no difference to my classmates. While it was a constant obsession with me, it apparently never entered their minds. When I wrote the article for the Washington Post telling how it was growing up a Nazarene – the strangeness I felt in not being able to dance, go to the movies, or play games that used dice – the friends who shared those good old days with me expressed shock at what I had written. They knew me as a popular student leader, with a sense of humor, a member of the Honor Society, first trombone in the band, a forward on the varsity basketball team, and an officer in the student government. It would have been nice to have known this then. I didn't. Instead, I went to school each day with the mark of the beast stamped clearly in the middle of my forehead.

My coming of age in the church brought not only a sense of being different, but also a sense of dread. A dread associated with what happened to those people who decided not to be different, but to go join the crowd.

As it was taught to me, they might have a grand old time here, but just you wait. They are going to get theirs when they cross over to the other side. There are only two paths, I was told. One is broad and attractive. It glitters and glows and a lot of folks choose that way. But it is the way that leads to destruction – eternal destruction, no less. The other way leads to life eternal. However, it is a narrow way, and few find it.

I was raised on this "good news of hell" as someone facetiously put it. Traveling evangelists came through our little town twice a year, and told harrowing tales about men and women who had resisted God's call and suffered tragic consequences. I remember a night when I lay awake for hours, imagining that I heard the wailing of the souls in hell. It was just the wind whistling around the corner of my bedroom, but to a nine-year-old kid, as steeped in hell fire preaching as I was – still under the influence of that night's revival service – wind wasn't high on my list of probable causes.

The dread of all dreads for me was, to put it in the language of my church in my day, "sinning away my day of grace." This was known as the "unpardonable sin." Using one of those open to question scripture texts, some preachers preached that one could become so inured to the gospel word that God would just go off and leave them alone. The way it was preached to me that fateful October night was that God could be calling you right now to come forward and repent of your sins, and five minutes from now, if you haven't responded, say, "That's it, buddy. No more Mr. Nice Guy for you. You can go to hell as far as I am concerned." It was never put that way – in those exact words – but that's the meaning of the unpardonable sin as it was preached to me.

That is why in that fall revival, when my twelve year old ears heard the evangelist say that God could be speaking to you (I heard me) at this very moment, and five minutes from now you will be off his call list, I got up from my seat next to my Dad and went up and knelt at the communion rail, known in those low church days as the altar or mourners' bench, and began to pray for the salvation of my never-dying soul.

I didn't stay there long, partly because the preacher kept preaching, and I began to feel foolish, kneeling there alone in front of the congregation. What could also have caused me to get up and return to my spot in the pew next to my father was accepting the truth of what the preacher had said, and concluding that if indeed I had "sinned away my day of grace" – although I had no idea what sin I could possibly have committed that would so anger God that He would turn his back on me – what good would it do for me to keep on praying. I vividly remember snuggling up next to my Dad and feeling no comfort in that closeness. It was God's closeness that mattered to me. Only that could protect me from hell's flames.

This cloud lifted a few weeks later, when I picked up one of my parents' books, titled, <u>Impressions</u>. In it I found a chapter on "Impressions from Below" that contained a section on the unpardonable sin, and my eyes locked onto this sentence: "If you are concerned about the unpardonable sin that is a sure sign that you haven't committed it." What a relief those words were, but it was a relief that couldn't last.

You see, in the Nazarene Church of my day, fear was the weapon of choice for those who were marching forward to Zion in the army of the Lord. An especially harsh taskmaster came to be the pastor of the Laurel, Delaware Church. He seemed to have not only a bulging catalogue of sins, but also an up close and personal understanding of what hell would be like. Why he felt it his Christian duty to fashion a small wooden plaque, picturing a big eyeball and the words, "the eye of the Lord is in everyplace, beholding the evil and the good," and tack it onto the wall above the commode in the church restroom, I have no idea.

The God of that plaque – a snooping, judging, damning God – is the God I heard the most about in those growing up years: a God who loved us, to be sure, but only to a point. And that point had to do with your behavior. The word grace was used a lot in sermons and in songs. But grace defined as God's unmerited love toward us, a grace that accepts us just as we are, and is not contingent on our faithfully keeping all ten of the commandments, is not the grace I heard preached. My soul was nurtured on notions of the eternal punishment that awaits all those who stray ever so slightly from the narrow way. I lived in fear of that great Judgment Day, when Gabriel's trump would herald the arrival of the Lord of the universe who would separate the sheep from the goats. What I most feared was the apocalyptic spin put on this that has made Tim LeHaye a very rich man with his best selling <u>Left Behind</u> series of books on the rapture. The rapture, according to the true believers, is when Jesus decides – rather God decides – that it is time for his second and last visit to earth. At that time, all the saints, both living and dead, will be "called up" to meet him in the air. The calling up will happen rather suddenly and unexpectedly. The Bible puts it this way: "Two shall be lying in bed. One will be taken, and the other left." In the movie version of "Left Behind", I understand that cars are driving along a freeway, and some are careening every which way, because the erstwhile drivers of those free wheeling vehicles have been spirited off to meet their Lord in the air.

So convinced was I of the truth of this rapture tale, and equally as convinced that I would be one of the ones left behind, I needed something to ease my anxiety level. If not that, at least something that would let me know that the feared day had not yet arrived, leaving me some time to get my house in order so that I might be one of those who would get "caught up" to go meet the Lord in the sky. There was a girl two years ahead of me in school. She was an only child whose parents doted on her. She was also very religious and very plain. Had she been a more gorgeous type, given to living the fast life, she would not have been suited to perform my rapture test. So, every school day I looked for her. If she were there, then we were still living in the pre-rapture period, and I could breathe a bit more easily.

Being different, being afraid – was what church meant to me a lot of the time during those early years. But if that were all there was to it, I would not be writing this, and, in all probability I would have to be listed as a former child of the church. However, there was more.

It was in church that I got the distinct impression that life had meaning. Yes, I was taught creationism before it had a name, and the way my teachers talked, Adam and Eve were very real people and Eden was a very real place. And some of those traveling evangelists who passed through town twice a year knew exactly where it was. Buried in the rubble of this primitive theology, though, was the word I heard about history being God's story; there was purpose to it. It all didn't just happen – this universe of ours – it was molded in the hands of a Divine creator.

So was I, I learned in church. Miss Moffett might teach me in biology that I was 98% water, but my church taught me that I was made in the image of God, "a little lower than the angels," as the Psalmist put it, but special, nonetheless. Superintendent Helm would look at me across his desk, give me the results of the I.Q. test I had taken, and then tell me that I had the ability to do anything I wanted. In church I would be told, "to whom much is given, much is required," and have read to me the parable of the talents, and I knew that God, like Mr. Helm, had high expectations for me.

In all the raving and ranting about sinning and the ultimate consequence of it – smoldering in an eternal hell – I heard something else. It was a word about the need for me to take my actions seriously, simply because there were pen-ultimate consequences to sinning: not the least being, fashioning your own hell here on earth.

However, church was not all doom and gloom for me. There were some painful and embarrassing moments, to be sure. Like the Saturday night I was forced to play my trombone at the street meeting our church held underneath the clock in front of Peoples Bank. Or that Sunday afternoon when I was led out into Laurel Lake to be baptized, and as I was being dunked the necessary three times, I heard not only the preachers words, "in the name of the father, the son and the holy ghost", but also the "hey Starnesys" that rained down on me from my classmates who had climbed up into the trees along the lakeshore to get a better look at these strange goings on.

There were other moments, though. Sitting in church with my parents and feeling cared for. Not just by them, but also by their God. Dr. Albert Schweitzer writes about sitting with his father in church when he was very young, and although he did not understand a word that was being said, the organ music and the sunlight filtering through the stained glass windows filled him with delight. In my church it was a piano I listened to instead of an organ, and the stained glass windows arrived just before I left home for college, but I understood fully the sentiments Schweitzer was conveying. In all honesty, as I grew older, I fought for my turn to stay home with Benton. Since Sunday dinner was such an important occasion, Sunday morning was Mama's time to stay home with Benton and get the meal ready. But, it was open season regarding the Sunday evening and the mid-week prayer services. And each of us children insisted that justice and fairness dictated that we all should have a chance to sit with Benton, not to mention a chance to hear Jack Benny or Fibber McGee and Molly.

The love/hate relationship I had with the church errs on the side of love. Sundays are the only days of the week I remember most vividly. Actually, Saturday nights need to be included in that total recall column. You see, Saturday nights were Sunday-get-ready-times. Shoes were polished as we listened to the Grand Ole Opry broadcast on WSM Nashville, and read the Sunday comics. Sunday clothes were set out – ironed, if necessary. Sunday dinners are the only meals I remember, and I can still rattle off the Sunday schedule of activities, including what radio shows we listened to. There was no game playing allowed – either inside or outside – in Nazarene homes, and no "secular" reading, which is why we read the Sunday comics on Saturday night. And yet those Sabbaths of long ago are not just looked at through nostalgically tinted glasses. It's my fondness for them at the time that has etched them in my memory.

Thirty years ago on an October Sunday morning, I preached a sermon titled, "I Choose the Church." That sermon was one of numerous attempts of mine to make a case for the church. The sermon began with a quote from an article I had just read in the "Christian Century" magazine, "Returning to the Fold: Disbelief Within the Community of Faith." The article was by Dr. Donald Miller, who, at the time, was professor of the sociology of religion at the University of Southern California. It is a statement of why, after years of non-involvement with the church, he returned. His doubts and questions remain, or as he put it: "I have given up on settling the question of the resurrection, whether Jesus was born of a virgin, whether he made the blind man see and the lame walk.... I remain agnostic on these issues of faith, but open." He spoke of the values of ritual and tradition and locating oneself in such a tradition, and then he said this:

> "One thing that brought me back to the church was asking simply: what are the alternatives to the church? Where are the communi-

ties that sanction the pursuit of meaning and truth as a legitimate enterprise? That have material and personal resources to assist in this search? That provide regular occasions for confession of failures? That renew and inspire? That provide a setting where children are nurtured? Where family members can be buried? Where births can be celebrated? Where social issues can be debated? There are a number of institutions that deal with one or several of these questions, but historically the church has demonstrated its ability to energize all of these activities."

I still choose the church. Its rituals and customs are so much a part of me. Its ancient prayers, even in this day, say it as well as it has ever been said. And its music – most of it anyway – often touches spots in me that nothing else can reach.

Last Sunday morning I did not go to church. Guests came and it wasn't convenient. A good enough reason, but something didn't feel right about not going. For, God's sake, I said to myself. I am seventy years old, been in church all my life, paid to be there most of the time, and why do I feel like I am skipping school? And why is it that I feel this way every Sunday morning that, for one reason or another, I choose to, as we say, "neglect the means of grace." Is it habit? Is it custom? That's certainly a part of it, with a little bit of sense of duty thrown in for good measure.

But that's not all there is to it. At least for me it isn't. And I am not sure I can put it into words. Simply stated, I continue to "choose the church" for the same reasons I laid out for that congregation of mine thirty years ago. The same reasons that Professor Miller listed in that "Christian Century" article of his I quoted earlier: the values of ritual and tradition, and the pursuit of meaning and truth. But even this isn't enough to fully explain my continuing to choose the church.

What gets in the way of my being able to articulate this faith I have in the institutional church, is that it is difficult, well nigh impossible, to put into words matters of the heart. Blaise Pascal talked about the heart having its reasons. He even said these are reasons that reason knows nothing about; and my still being a member of Christ's holy church has more to do with heart than with head.

Bessie Woody, in her early nineties, was on a list of about one hundred of my church's shut-in members. These were persons who were confined to either their home or a health care facility. I had two associates and the three of us would divide this list up among us, and twice a year visit each one and serve them the sacrament of Holy Communion. Being the senior minister of this very large church meant that my schedule was full most of the time.

When I got to the nursing home that had been home to Bessie for about ten years, I was running late for another appointment, so I decided to leave out a prayer that comes early on in the ritual. I got the first word out of my mouth – the word that follows on the heels of the prayer I had omitted – and I felt Bessie's hand on my knee. I also heard her begin to pray the prayer I had chosen to skip over,

> "We do not presume to come to this thy table,
>
> O merciful Lord
>
> Trusting in our own righteousness, …"

I joined in the prayer with her, determined to read every last word of the ritual, however long it took.

When I prayed the last prayer, saying what was for me the final amen, and made the beginnings of a move to get up, I felt Bessie's hand on my knee again, and this time she began singing,

"Have Thine own way, Lord, have Thine own way,

Thou art the potter, I am the clay.

Mold me and make me, after Thy will,

While I am waiting, yielded and still."

When we finished singing, she told me that when Dr. Rustin had been her pastor for so many years at Mt. Vernon Place Church in Washington, D. C., he closed every communion service with the singing of that hymn. Dr. Rustin was long since dead, and Mt. Vernon Place Church was struggling to stay alive in downtown D.C., yet the week in week out influence of that pastor and that church lived on in Bessie Woody as she whiled away lonely hours in her "nursing" home, buoyed by the faith she nurtured at a communion rail years and years ago. The heart has its reasons.

Ralph LaPore was not a member of my church. He was a Roman Catholic, but Margaret and Ellen, his wife and daughter, both members, asked me to stop by the house and visit Ralph. He had lung cancer and was near death. I sat on the edge of his bed, talking most of the time with Margaret as Ralph drifted in and out of consciousness. As she and I were talking, Ralph mumbled something. It made no sense to me, however, Margaret, having spent long years with him, said, "He's trying to say the 'Hail Mary.'" He did it a couple more times.

That triggered a tape in my head that was recorded twenty-five years earlier. When I was in college I worked in the meat department of a super market in Boston, and every Saturday night Archbishop Cushing would say the Hail Mary and the Our Father for fifteen minutes over station WBZ. For four years, every Saturday night, that gravelly voice hammered into my head the words that I began to speak into Ralph's ear.

> "Hail Mary, full of grace, the Lord is with thee,
>
> Blessed are thou among women,
>
> And blessed is the fruit of thy womb, Jesus.
>
> Holy Mary, mother of God, pray for us sinners,
>
> Now and at the hour of our death"

I kept repeating that and Ralph drifted off to sleep. The heart has its reasons.

Years ago I decided to preach a sermon on the subject of grace. I did what I usually do when putting a sermon together, check out the notebooks I have kept to see what I have noted about a particular subject. What seemed strange to me then was that I had no notes about any grace sermon I had ever read. Curious about this, I decided to check some of the sermon books in my library. None of the pulpit masters of my time – Fosdick, Buttrick, Read, Kennedy, Hamilton – had ever preached a sermon on grace. At least any published in the books of theirs that I had read. They used the word a lot. But nowhere did I find a whole sermon given over to the subject of grace.

I ended up preaching on grace the next Sunday. And I began the sermon with a disclaimer – maybe grace is too big a word to reduce to words. I told the congregation that as far as I knew Jesus never preached a sermon on grace. He told stories about it. I told those people that day that his greatest grace story, for me at least, is the one he told about the Prodigal Son. Then I told them a few other grace stories I had read and told them one of my own. Some words are just too big for words, I said, and grace just might be one of them.

So is church for me. When I want to tell someone why I still choose the church; why after all these years of looking at it from the inside out; why, after witnessing all the sinfulness, the hypocrisy – a lot of it my own – do I still seat myself in a pew every Lord's day morning, I have to tell stories. About the little frame church – now brick – in Cowan, Tennessee, that my dad staggered into one night, and walked out with head held high carrying along with him a new lease on life. Or I tell about the time I walked forward myself, knelt down, and as best as an eight year old child can do, promised God that I would do my best to walk in his way. If the time is right, and the questioner deserving, I will tell the story of my gay son, sitting in the choir, during a communion service, trying his damndest to come to terms with this alleged – by some in the church -- abomination, yet, for him, who he was, and hearing the celebrant quote those wonderful words from a Paul Tillich sermon: "You are accepted by God. Just as you are. Accept the fact that you are accepted." He did, and he walked out of church that day a new person, who in neither his eyes, nor God's, was abominable. I thrill to tell the story of laying my hands on my daughter's head as she was ordained a minister in the United Methodist Church. All those years she saw me drink to excess, openly eviscerate congregants at the dinner table, and color the air around me blue with a choice word or two. Still in all, she, too, chooses the church. And how many stories could I tell about the times while sitting in church I have sensed the goodness and greatness of it all. Like the Sunday not long ago. I was sitting with my twin grandchildren, Hannah and Jacob. When we stood and began to sing,

> "Let us with a joyful mind praise our God forever kind,
>
> Rich in mercies that endure, ever faithful, ever sure."

I looked down at those two precious gifts standing next to me, in God's house, singing about a faithfulness of God that their ten-year-old minds haven't yet fully understood, and the only thing I could do, like my father before me had done when confronted with God's amazing grace, was to let the tears flow.

So to Herb, Gerry, and other friends of mine from those early Nazarene days, who wonder how, and why, I have held on to this faith of mine that "the Church is of God and will be preserved until the end of time," all I can say is: these are my stories and I'm sticking to them, because my heart has its reasons.

Chapter 4

"In New England Stands a College Near Blue Quincy Bay"
Mann and Summerscales

It follows, I suppose, child of the church that I was, that I would chose a church college. And since church for me meant the Nazarene Church, my choice of college would be one of theirs.

The Nazarene Church was divided into educational zones, and Eastern Nazarene College in Quincy, Massachusetts, was the school for my area of the country. Not all of the seven Nazarene Colleges were academically accredited, so ENC, having received its seal of approval from the New England Association of Colleges and Secondary Schools, caused it to be perceived by some as the one with the most rigorous academic standards. I am pleased that this was the case, since the education I received there stood me in such good stead in the graduate schools that followed. But I knew nothing of all this when I started making my plans to go there. All I knew was that I wanted to go to college – to my church's college – and ENC was the one that was in my educational zone.

It was also the one that I had heard about over the years. Beginning as a dream of establishing a "holiness" college, growing just enough to purchase the Adams mansion and grounds along Quincy Bay, and then continuing to grow by cultivating its constituent churches in New England, New York, Pennsylvania, Ohio, Maryland, and Delaware. Every summer, the college sent out male quartets to sing in the Nazarene churches in the zone. Accompanied by a school administrator who would give a pitch about the college and also preach, the groups would sing, solicit pledges to the college building program, and recruit potential students. Whenever these quartets came to my little church, I dreamed of one day singing in just such a group.

My sister Jane was the first member of our family to go to college. Since financial aid, either from home or the college, was out of the question, she worked for a year at the local DuPont plant, saving enough to put her through the first year at ENC. She did well academically, as she had during all her years of school, but decided to leave after her freshman year and return home to work. Since Jane so wanted an advanced degree, and since she possessed then, and still does, the ability to stretch dollars further than any of the rest of us Starnes children, I have always felt that there was more to her leaving college than just the fact that she ran out of money. Since I have never been able to see clearly into my own motivations, I will not attempt to parse my sister's personality.

What she brought home with her were stories of college life, and a yearbook. Thumbing through the pages of the "Nautilus," with its candid shots of activities – all involving "true believers" like me – and those marvelous male quartets, it became increasingly obvious that Eastern Nazarene College is where I would end up.

And so it was on a day in late August 1950, that I walked down the front steps of the little "transitional" house my father had rented to head toward Boston and Eastern Nazarene College. When Elizabeth, Jane and Ruth all married within a year's time, Daddy concluded that the Bethel house – the one I loved and still dream about – was too big. What really scared him was that the three girls – board payers all – getting married and moving out, would make it difficult for him to meet the $27.50 mortgage payment. It also moved things along, when he was offered $12,000 – an unheard of price for a Bethel house – as well as a tremendous return on his $3500 investment of just four years earlier. He took the unheard of offer, and bought a new house in Laurel. However, after two years there, he put that house on the market. The pull back to Bethel was more than he could withstand. There wasn't any house available that met his requirements, so he rented this small house until he could find one that suited him.

My memories of that day are sketchy. I can see Lucille, my sister, now married, standing on the front steps of that little house, waving to me. I don't remember Mama being there. She could have been inside crying, because three years later, when I was leaving to go back to college for my final year, she was sitting in the kitchen, by the back door of the house Daddy finally found that suited him, and she was crying. I asked her what was wrong. She said she hated to see me leave, because now she had no one to talk to. My brother Benton – her constant care – had died, but Daddy was still there, and so was her darling baby whose 14 year-old curls she still kept tucked away in an envelope. Maybe I was special to her. I bore her Dad's name – Thomas Cowan. I was the "spitting image" of her brother, Robert. So, it's not hard for me to imagine that she was in the house crying as the brand new Chevrolet Fleetline, sporting General Motors first power glide transmission, pulled out of the drive, carrying me, my Dad, my brother Luther, and our pastor, Brother Mayberry, who would not only help with the driving, but navigate the way through New York City. My one memory of that long ride is my father asking me why I thought college was necessary. If I offered a response before he added, "DuPont has been good enough for the rest of the family," I don't recall it.

I have wondered about this. There is no question that at some level my Dad was pleased with my decision to go to college. He loved to tell others about his boy being "off at school," and he, no doubt, saw this as my way of fulfilling his often stated desire that I "would make something of myself." He did harbor some suspicions about college boys, as he would call them, who had come to DuPont to work in supervisory positions. Maybe he was conflicted about college, the result, perhaps, of his never having gone away to school, unlike his "more successful" younger brother. It might simply have been a control issue, since all his other children had never wandered too far from his watchful eye. Where I have chosen to leave it after years of therapy – is that my father supported me as best he could. Never once did he stand in my way. And even as he asked me why I was going, he was taking me there, and, in his own way, wishing me well.

The picture in my head of that day that has never faded is the one of me in my dorm room, alone. Daddy, Luther, and Brother Mayberry have left for home. I am sitting on the trunk that holds all that could be called mine, and three thoughts have crowded everything else out of my mind: I am farther away from home than I have ever been; I know absolutely no one here; and the $182 in my pocket – saved after a summer of shift work at the DuPont plant – is all the money I have, and won't cover my first semester's expenses. The rest of that day is a mishmash of things that I know happened – meeting my roommate and a few others, some of whom have been life long friends – but no clear memory of anything else other than sitting on my trunk feeling very much alone in the world.

The anxiety lessened as I became more acclimated to these new surroundings. The college business office was helpful in locating a part time job for me in a super market. Working in the meat department of the Acme Store in Laurel, not only taught me how to cut meat, it had also made me a member of the Amalgamated Meat Cutters Union. This union card saw to it that I was paid almost twice the minimum hourly rate. Advisors helped with arranging my classes. All was going well.

I loved ENC. It was just the place for me. Going to the University of Delaware would have been too much of an adjustment for me – I am not sure I would have survived that immersion into the real world. And I would have found myself still fighting those same old battles of making excuses for my church's mandatory rules of behavior. But, here, at this holiness college, I was one of them. These were my kind of people. No longer was I "different." Everybody here, or so it seemed to me, was a Nazarene. Nobody asked me if I had seen the latest movie. I didn't have to hide from an upper class girl because someone told me she was going to ask me to the prom. Those prom days were over. And the church – my church – was not on the other side of the tracks. Here we were mainline. Those days of standing on the outside and looking in were over. Finally, I belonged. What I did not know, however, was that in coming to college, I had taken a step in the direction of the faith that would eventually lead me out of this church that had brought new life to my Dad and, in turn, to his family.

A part of that step was the classes. Meeting the academic requirements was a challenge, to say the least. I had taken academic courses in high school – French, Latin, Algebra, Geometry, Chemistry – and done very well. But I was not a reader and had never written a research paper. When my professors passed out reading assignments and mid term test dates – a month and a half away – my initial reaction was to say, no sweat, and head for the gym and shoot some baskets. I did not know how to study – a fact that became agonizingly clear when that month and a half sped by so rapidly; ending long before I had finished the reading, resulting in my receiving my first ever D.

Being a rather quick study it didn't take long for me to begin to develop some study habits that have guided me through to this day. It certainly did not hurt that about this time I met the girl who, a few years later, would agree to spend the rest of her life with me. Two things attracted me to her at the freshman reception: name and looks – in that order. When they called her name, Waveline Trout, I nudged Joe Williamson, standing next to me, and said, "What a fishy name. Wave – Line – Trout." We laughed and I looked and that was that. Wave Trout also knew how to study. Afternoons found her in the library, not on the basketball court. She became my mentor as well as my lover.

And I began to love what I studied. My selected major was philosophy and the questions started bubbling. "How do we know what we know?" "Is that tree real, or is my idea of the tree reality?" "If a man is hungry, and he steals a loaf of bread to feed his family, has he broken one of the commandments?" We make jokes about out of touch with reality professors who sit around and debate such things as "How many angels can dance on the head of a pin." But to someone like me – raised in a world of right and wrong, black and white, true and false – it was freeing to hear it suggested – by those who shared my faith, even – that determining what was right and what was wrong, or what was true and what was false, wasn't as easy a task as some might think. In ethics classes, we were also left with the distinct impression that quite often life has to be lived in the gray areas.

I especially loved the literature courses. Hawthorne's <u>Scarlet Letter</u> forced me to look, maybe for the first time, at the harsh, unforgiving spirit that all too often captures orthodox religions. George Eliot's, <u>Adam Bede</u>, especially that scene where the newborn baby is hidden under a woodpile, and as the mother walks away the lengthening distance doesn't drown out the baby's cries. No evangelist ever told me any story about living with the consequences of our actions that matched that one. John Bunyan's, <u>Pilgrim's Progress</u>, gave me my first notion that the religious quest was a lifelong process. It was more than just a matter of being "saved" and later "sanctified, and that would be the end of that. No, it's a life long trip – this journey of faith – and there are plenty of valleys and shadows along the way. Reading Shakespeare's tragedies chipped away further at what I had been taught about the rather easy way we can determine the good guys and the bad guys, not to mention any notion that life is ever a romp through the woods.

As is most often the case with classes, it's the professors who make the difference, and my life at ENC was enriched by some very good ones. There were the young ones who were working on their doctoral studies in Boston's universities. Wilbur Mullen was one of these. He taught philosophy, and in an easy going, thoughtful way, let me know that doubts and questions had major roles to play in the building of a strong faith. This was a first for me. All my life, preachers preached and we listened. If one of these spokespersons for God said that Joshua commanded the sun to stand still, no one close to me ever raised an objection. But, here, at this Nazarene College, Professor Mullen let me know, it was okay to raise questions. In later years, I understand, he said that all he wanted on his tombstone was his name, the dates marking his time here on earth, and the one word, "philosopher".

Dean Bertha Munro was not one of the young professors on campus. She had been at ENC from its beginning. An honors graduate at Radcliffe College, she taught literature. True to the holiness tradition, she nonetheless introduced us to literature of all types – modern as well as ancient. Her 19th Century Prose, Literature by Types, and

Shakespeare classes are three of the most challenging courses I have ever taken. Quite apart from the course material she presented, was the life she lived. She came closest to living the holy life the Nazarene Church proclaimed as the standard as any one I ever met. She, too, welcomed questions, and never feared that her exposing us to great literature – sometimes looking at the seamy side of life – was undermining our faith.

Professor Spangenberg, another of the oldies, I include here – as a part of my faith journey – because I credit her with teaching me how to construct a sermon. Her course in non-fiction writing was the best sermon construction course I ever took. That course had nothing to do with preaching, but her three basic principles of writing have stayed with me: make an outline, have some idea where you want this piece to go, and pre-paper thought. How she stressed that last one. Before you put pen to paper, she would say, let your conscious and your sub-conscious stew on the idea. And when you finally get down to writing, cut, cut, cut. Don't waste words. Simplify. I loved her.

Then there were the preachers who came to speak in chapel and hold revival services. They were unlike any I had ever heard. Well educated, gifted speakers – most of them anyway – their sermons evidenced not just blind obedience to the faith, but reasoned thinking as well.

There were even "non-believers" on campus, of all things. Not many. Just enough to let us "true believers" know that there was still a world out there. These were pre-hippy days, but some of these fit that classification. They operated on the edges – at least the edges of Nazarenedom. And they were some of the brightest and most interesting persons on campus. Dean Munro, by her own admission, was especially drawn to these Bohemian types. She confessed to a friend of mine – a favorite of hers, dismissed in his senior year for smoking – that she always liked the bad ones.

College opened up the world "out there" to me. Boston was just a short subway ride away – a ten-cent trip that introduced me to symphonies, art galleries and nice restaurants, as well as to Fenway Park and the Boston Garden. Working in the meat room of Supreme Market called all my previous stereotypes into question. These were, obviously, godless people. Frank Broll, standing at the butcher block in front of me, would break forth into song, "I'm in the nude for love." If he weren't singing some of his porno lyrics, he would be flailing away at the pork chops in front of him, and cursing Betty Furness, the television spokesperson in those days for General Electric appliances. Chopping harder and harder, he would say, "that goddamn broad opens and closes refrigerator doors, and makes 100 grand a year. I freeze my balls off in here for a lousy $100 a week." Frank Fall would come to work after working the night shift at the fire house, and as he walked through the wrapping room where the women were putting the meat into packages to be sent up stairs to the floor, he would goose one of them on the way by. The later to be called sexually abused person would, more often than not, giggle, and tell him to keep his frigging hands off her ass.

These same "godless" people would, on Saturday evenings, grow quiet for fifteen minutes as they listened to their beloved Archbishop Cushing say the rosary and the Hail Mary. One day, Johnny Lentini, with tears in his eyes, showed me the indulgence he had just purchased for his mother, and explained this whole process that Martin Luther condemned and helped kick off the Protestant Reformation. Peter Sullivan did not ridicule me when I came to work one Ash Wednesday and commented on the dark smudges I had seen on peoples' foreheads. I had never heard of Ash Wednesday, and Peter gave me my first lesson on church liturgy.

These "godless" souls, as I had been taught, became anything but "godless" in my sight. They repeatedly asked me how I was doing. The women who could swear with the best of them, fretted over me, and reminded me to take care of myself and make sure I ate right. They became my friends, and my last day there before I left for graduation and marriage they threw a going away party for me. Mr. Cifrino, one of the owners, sent liquor down from the package store upstairs. He even came down, and joined in the toast they all gave me, along with some money they had collected, and a card signed "from your friends in the meat room" with a reference to a popular song at the time, "Three Coins in the Fountain." I even joined in the toast, letting the first ever drop of whiskey touch my lips. I had come so far in just four years in college that I did not think God would strike me dead for just being kind, figuring that he might even conclude that this was one time that it would not have been such a good idea to "come out from among them and be ye separate."

As I write this, Wave and I have just returned from a Homecoming weekend at ENC. Our first trip back was in 1993, almost forty years after we graduated. We weren't aware of it at the time, but this was a self-imposed exile. We had this notion that because we had left the Nazarene Church – "backslidden" in some people's eyes – our welcome would have been anything but warm. There was some evidence supporting this conclusion of ours, since neither of us, even though we had both been one of the big men and one of the big women on campus had ever been asked to serve on any alumni board.

In 1993, there was the 50th anniversary of the A Cappella Choir. I had sung in the choir for two years and I wanted to see some of my old friends. It was a great time. We saw old friends and shared stories – it was just as if we had never left. Then two years ago Wave and I each received a Lifetime Achievement Award. We were the first non-Nazarenes to receive this honor.

A part of this year's homecoming weekend was a gathering of the men and women who had traveled in summer groups representing the college. Having traveled for three summers, achieving my boyhood ambition to be in a college quartet, I was invited back. There were about a hundred of us seated in the choir loft of the College Church. I was sitting next to Bob Montgomery who sang first tenor in the Gospelaires – my first quartet that traveled in the summer of 1951. Wave was in the audience, sitting next to two friends from the dorm room down the hall, one of whom she hadn't seen for fifty years. It's not the same church building where she and I worshipped. In some ways it isn't even the same college. The night before we had attended the drama departments fall production, "Guys and Dolls." We laughed at the selection of this particular play. In our day, plays, like movies, were on the "not to do list." Now, sitting in a fine arts center theater, built with Nazarene dollars, named after Edith Cove, one of those early "saints" of ENC, we were watching dancing, drinking, crap shooting and even spoofing of Salvation Army lads and lassies. And walking across the campus, you saw your share of spiked, sometimes amber, hair, and an occasional belly button ring.

But as I looked at Wave out there in a spot not far from the one where I first laid eyes on her, and a blue grass group was beautifully singing a gospel song I grew up on,

> "O, they tell me of a home far beyond the skies,
>
> O, they tell me of a home far away.
>
> O, they tell me of a place where no storm clouds rise,
>
> O, they tell me of an unclouded day."

"Guys and Dolls," spiked hair, or belly button rings were the farthest things from my mind. Seated just to the left of Wave was Dr. Mann, or, as we called him, "Prexy." At age 95 he needs a walker to get around. In my minds eye though, he is still that ramrod straight Vermonter who was such a stabilizing influence on my young life. Down a few rows in front of him sat Audrey Ward. A smile was on her face as she listened to the group singing not only about that "unclouded day," but also about a Land of Beulah "where the flowers bloom forever, and the sun is always bright." Just a few years younger than "Prexy" it wasn't hard for me to imagine that her soul's eyes were already fixed on that "land that is fairer than day, which by faith we can see from afar." Audrey Ward brought grace to the college business office. Without those extra few days – sometimes weeks – she consistently gave me to come up with the tuition payments due, the $182 I brought along from home in my pocket never would have been anything more than a forfeited deposit on a college education.

As I sat in that choir loft, I wasn't thinking about how much ENC has changed since those early 1950 days. Rather, I was thinking about how indebted I am to this small, relatively unknown, college. It brought Wave into my life, as well as some friends who have been sojourners with me along the way. It is also where, in starts and stops, my own faith began to develop legs of its own.

Chapter 5

"He made some pastors, ..."

I opened my eyes that late May morning in 1954 enveloped in a feeling words can't describe. Ecstasy might be a bit strong, but not by much. Commencement exercises were just a few hours away, and barring being yanked out of the academic processional, or given a blank diploma because of unpaid tuition or library fines, the end was near. College had not been easy. It wasn't the course work that made those four years a struggle. Once I developed some study habits, the classes – most of them anyway – were, in some instances, exciting, and in all cases mind expanding. No, it was working thirty, sometimes forty, hours a week in Supreme Market, all the while determined to finish in four years. It was not wanting to give up my beloved game of basketball, or to go off singing with quartets on weekends or with the college choir during spring breaks. And without giving anything up, I had done it, in four years, paying every last dime of my education myself. There were no Latin words after the name on my diploma, as there were on Wave's, but I did finish as a member of the honor society and on the Dean's List.

Mama and Daddy made the trip to Boston. Luther came along, able to finesse his own graduation from high school. Florine was the only sister who couldn't make it. The other four were there with their husbands. Daddy had threatened to give his favorite shout – "Well I say glory" – as I crossed the stage to receive my diploma, but he didn't. I used to cringe when he would go public with his faith, like the time, serving as president of the very first Parent Teachers' Association meeting in Laurel School, he opened that inaugural session with a prayer. Saying "glory" in the midst of a bunch of shouting Nazarenes would not have been all that embarrassing, but I was relieved that he didn't.

Neither of our families was happy with the way Wave and I had arranged the events of graduation week. The scheduling of graduation was not our doing; the scheduling of our wedding for the Saturday after Monday's graduation most certainly was.

Logistics was uppermost in my family's mind. It was out of the way to leave Boston, return home to Delaware, and then load up again and head for Ohio and the wedding. Wave's family's concerns were much more substantive. Having already given five daughters away to the ones who had promised to love, honor and cherish them, my parents didn't find the prospect of sending another child off to married bliss all that troubling. This was not the case with Wave's parents. Not only was this a road less traveled for them, this was a road they had never been on.

Wave was the first of two children born to Floyd and Beulah, a precious gift to them – especially to her father. He named her after a little girl he had once known in the southern Ohio town where he was raised. She was always Daddy's little girl. It was never any question that she would go to college. A champion debater in high school, delegate to Girls' State numerous times, an honor student, a successful future for her was always assumed.

However, her parents' college of choice for her was Kent State – just a few miles from home. But Wave had other plans for her life. She was actively involved in the Barberton, Ohio Church of the Nazarene, and her young pastor, whom she dearly loved, had attended ENC. Like me she had also been exposed to the quartets as they made their summer rounds. So, much to her parents' dismay, she did as they had schooled her to do – made up her own mind – and headed off to Boston to meet me.

Certainly, they must have thought, after graduation she will come home to Ohio and to us, at least for a while. But no, love turns one's head; now she would never be coming home, ever again, as their darling little girl. Our wedding pictures – at least the one showing the two sets of parents standing like sentries on either side of the happy couple – tell this particular tale best. My parents have rather pleasant expressions on their faces. Wave's parents, on the other hand, look as though they are standing beside an open casket.

There is an added dimension to Wave's parents' disquiet – especially her father's. His daughter, the one for whom he has had such great plans, is marrying a preacher-to-be, of all things. Floyd Trout was not a deeply religious man, in any formalized sense; meaning, he had rather serious doubts about the institutional church. He would go, occasionally, to satisfy Beulah, or if Wave had a part in some church performance. But he was not your every Sunday worshipping type. Being the simple, honorable man that he was, living by the prophet Micah code – doing justice, loving mercy, and walking humbly – he had no time for those who lived one way during the week and another way on Sundays.

He also had rather serious suspicions about preachers. He had seen some good ones, like Bob Shoff, and the one that married Beulah and him. For the most part, though, in his eyes the Elmer Gantry types were in the decided majority. More even than the morality issue, was the economic one. One of his sisters had married a preacher, and their life was one long struggle of trying to make ends meet. He wanted more for the pride of his life. But we were in love, and, except for a couple brief periods of my wondering if this were the real thing, had gone steady for our four years of college. We wanted to be married, and we were.

The marriage ceremony is a hazy memory, at best. I remember scurrying all over Akron the morning of the wedding trying to locate a pair of small black shoes for one of the ring bearers. I remember being insufferably warm on an early June scorcher, in a non air-conditioned church, and almost passing out, both from the heat and my own anxiety, as I sang, while Wave and I knelt, "O Jesus We have Promised." I remember Wave and me standing behind a table filled with wedding gifts, at the reception, and saying to her, "How on earth are we going to get all this stuff back to Boston," and she, rather sultrily, says back to me, "How on earth could you be thinking of something like that at a time like this?"

We drove off from the church in my father's new 1953 Chevrolet. One of those "see how time flies" moments happened to me not long ago, when I saw a similar car to the one that took us off on our very first ride as husband and wife, and as it passed, I spotted the "antique automobile" wording on its license plates.

It does seem a long time ago – that first night in the Statler Hotel in downtown Cleveland. Cleveland, along with Philadelphia, gets made the butt of jokes. "The first prize is a week in Cleveland. And the second prize is two weeks in Cleveland." But, for me, Cleveland will always be special. We drove back through Ohio to load up all the stuff that was on that wedding reception table, and headed south to Washington, D. C. To this day, whenever someone mentions the Army/McCarthy hear-

Through Fear to Faith

ings, Wave will say, "that's where Tom took me on our honeymoon." Those who know her best will smile when she says this. Truth is, we were both political news junkies, and had she really not wanted to be there, we would not have been. It was a swelteringly hot summer day as we stood in a crowded, non air-conditioned, senate office building, and heard Joseph Welch say those famous five words of his, "Senator, have you no shame?"

We still weren't sure how all this marital bounty would make its way to Boston. It didn't take long for my father to convince us that we needed a car, and further to convince us that his favorite Chevrolet dealer would have just the car for us. Our first major purchase as husband and wife was a 1950 Buick Special, low mileage, which my Dad helped us get by co-signing a note at Sussex Trust Company. It was the first of a long list of note signings for Wave and me, and with a new car filled with housekeeping items, we headed back to ENC for more school.

The "more school" would be for me. ENC had a postgraduate course specifically designed for those preparing to enter the ministry. Since the Nazarene Church did not make seminary education a requirement for ordination, the bachelor of theology graduate degree ENC offered would educationally qualify those wanting to become ministers. There were economic security reasons for this move back to Boston: both of us had jobs there. Wave would begin her teaching career at a school on Cape Cod, and I would continue working in Supreme Market's meat room as I took courses preparing me for my life as a minister in the Church of the Nazarene.

Exactly when the ministry became my chosen career path remains a mystery. No "burning bush" or "road to Damascus" experience suggested that preaching might be what God wanted me to do with my life. The best answer I have ever been able to give to the inevitable question, asked by denominational review boards, "would you tell us about your call to ministry," was never more than something on the order of telling my inquisitors that there was never any specific time; that it was more or less, an emerging notion that perhaps this is what God would want me to do. I longed to be able to say something a bit more dramatic: something about a voice or maybe even a sign from heaven. But all I could ever do was talk of a growing feeling, making it sound as if I was describing my sexual awakening. It is fair to say that however indistinct my call was to me, the questions about its validity came later. When I finished that year at ENC, I was ready to take the next step in preparing for the parish ministry.

That next step for most of my ENC friends, whose career paths were also leading toward the ministry, was seminary. Trimming my sails a bit, I decided to take seminary in small doses. For one thing, I wanted a break from being a full time student as well as an almost full time worker. I also wanted to go to work in a church. An offer came from a church near Pittsburgh, but I chose to accept a position as assistant minister in Wave's home church in Barberton, Ohio. It was a large church – as Nazarene churches go – and I liked the pastor. What also helped in making this decision was Wave receiving a teaching position in her hometown high school. She was thrilled to return to this place that had given her so much, and more even than that, to take her place as a peer with teachers and administrators she cared so much about. Though I don't recall thinking it at the time, returning the wandering daughter to the arms of her parents was not an unwise move. If they had to have a preacher for a son-in-law, an Ohio preacher might be the best they could hope for.

As a part of planning the move to Ohio, I applied and was accepted at Oberlin College's Graduate School of Theology. Oberlin College, located in the Western Reserve, an area just west of Cleveland, was well known for its Ivy League quality education, and its decidedly liberal bias. Equally well known was its Graduate School of Theology; not just for its liberal slant on things theological, but for its outstanding faculty as well. I enrolled in two seminars that fall semester: philosophy of religion and a history of the Reformation. It was the first dip of my toes in liberal waters. Looking back on it in later years, I came to see it as my first move – not really a move; more like a feint – out of the Nazarene Church.

What going to Oberlin meant was that for the first time in my life, I was exposed to professors who were committed to "THE faith" as opposed to professors who were committed to "OUR faith." Both Dr. Wolff and Dr. Lee were "believers", in the traditional sense. Dr. Lee had graduated from another one of the Nazarene colleges. Each class session was opened with a prayer. And one day, Dr. Wolff began a class by saying "I want all of you who believe in intercessory prayer to join me in praying for the child of one of our students who is seriously ill." And he, in what I perceived as very un-Lutheran like, got down on his knees in good Nazarene fashion and prayed the kind of prayer that I had heard prayed so often in my little holiness church back home – a prayer for the healing of a child.

This was new to me. Obviously, this was a Christian seminary – preparing, in those days, men for the ministry – but there were no forbidden questions. There was no house doctrine to defend. Furthermore, not just a few of these tweedy sorts, pedaling their bikes around this little New England look-alike town, puffed away on their briars.

On Tuesdays, I would be back at my post as assistant pastor of the Barberton Nazarene Church. Reverend Baxter took me with him on pastoral calls, dropping little hints as we rode along on how one went about plying this preaching trade. Since part of my job description was serving as secretary – a part I never remember hearing verbalized in the hiring process – he force-fed me on learning to type and to cut a stencil. The hunt and peck system of typing that I learned, by necessity, I am still using even as I am hunting and pecking my way through this very sentence. Paul Baxter finally got a secretary after I left. It proved to be his undoing. She was the married daughter of a prominent church family, and she and Paul fell in love. Both left their families to start a new life together, and Paul left the ministry. He died at an early age, finishing his career as a counselor for troubled youth. I don't know how the people at the Barberton church remember Paul Baxter, if they remember him at all. In the church records, it is noted that he was there when the beautiful new church that now stands out on the edge of town was built. I hope he gets credit for that. What I remember him for is giving me the best course in what is now called "practics" in seminary curricula that I ever had, and it is no stretch when I tell people that Paul Baxter taught me how to spend my days as a preacher.

There was never any question that this was the career path I was on: and not just any pastor. I was in the early stages of a career as a Nazarene pastor. The classes at Oberlin pulled back the shades a bit on the windows of my mind, but never enough to raise any doubts that this particular community of faith that had brought me this far along in my journey would be my faith home forever.

So, I began my ascendancy on the church's equivalent of the corporate ladder. Since I had traveled with ENC quartets throughout the Akron District of the church for three summers, mine was a recognizable face. I was given a position as Director of Teenage Ministries on the Akron District, and invited to join a local group of clergy that played golf on Mondays during the warm months, and handball at the YMCA during the cold months. I even came within a few votes of being elected to a national youth board, something that has caused me to wonder on occasion, if those few votes had gone my way, would that early elevation have turned my head and altered the course of my life.

What did alter the course of my life was Wave's pregnancy. Barberton Church paid me subsistence wages. As long as Wave was teaching, we were able to live quite well. But twenty-five dollars a week, even in 1956, was not enough to meet the basic needs of a family of two. The Akron District Superintendent knew me very well; I had roomed with his son my senior year in college. It was clear in my mind that I had told him I wanted a church of my own. So much so that the Barberton Church gave Wave and me a farewell reception, presenting us with a lovely eight place setting of china – which we still use. My heart sank when I approached Dr. Taylor at the district assembly and asked him where my church would be, and he said, "why, Tom, I didn't know you wanted a church." My father's faith in God's faithfulness – we will get what we need – was not even in its infancy stage with me at this point in my life. But it worked for me, nonetheless, proving, at least to my satisfaction, that God's faithfulness, quite often, is operative apart from either our belief or our unbelief.

It worked in the person of Ken Pearsall. Ken had been the vice-president of ENC when I was there. With his portfolio tilted heavily in the direction of institutional development, most of his summers were spent traveling with the quartets. Due to the forced intimacy of these tours – five adult males compressed into a single car and sleeping in crowded quarters – meant that Ken and I had come to know each other quite well. During my senior year, he accepted a call to pastor the First Church of the Nazarene in Akron – the largest church on the district. His wife, Ruth, had died leaving him with three small children, and after his marriage to her sister, Ruby, he decided that the needs of his children and those of his new wife could best be met by giving up his life on the road. Also pushing him in the direction of parish ministry was his love of preaching. Ken approached me when he heard that I had been left hanging, and asked me to come to First Church and be his assistant.

Here is where the story line in my head comes to a screeching halt. Of, course I accepted. I had a great deal of respect for Ken, and he could, like Paul Baxter, continue to show me how you live out this preacher's life. Although being mentored by one of the best was important to me, in all honesty, up there near the top on my list of reasons to take the position were the economic benefits offered. Instead of twenty-five dollars a week, I would get forty-five, plus an apartment. With daughter Vicky due to arrive in late October, this would position us well above the poverty level.

What I draw the blank on is why in telling Ken I would gladly accept his offer, I added a provision: I could only do this for six months, since I planned to enter the Nazarene Seminary for the second semester beginning the following January. When and why did I decide to do that?

I remember letters and calls from my ENC friends who had gone there directly from college asking me when I was coming out to join them. I have the vaguest recollection of a conversation with somebody, and that somebody said something like, "Well, if you have to go to seminary, you ought to go to our church's seminary."

Ken agreed to my terms and it was one of the happiest six-month periods in my life. Akron First was a great old church, filled with more than its share of wonderful people —some of whom came close to living the life of heart holiness — the Nazarene church doctrine that gave me the most difficulty, and precipitated my move into the Methodist Church. My work on the district continued, as did my golfing and handball playing. I was enjoying being a Nazarene pastor – especially one of the pastors, albeit the assistant, of a large church.

Adding to the joy – perhaps making the joy – of that six month stay at First Church was the birth of Victoria Jane, One of the very clear images in my head is of our very first nursery set up in the front room of that downstairs apartment next door to the church. Tennessee Ernie Ford had a single out, "First Born," a 45 rpm disc that I bought and played over and over again during those inexorably slow pre-birth months. Then when we brought her home from Akron General Hospital, I would sit in her nursery corner, rocking her to sleep as Tennessee Ernie sang in the background,

"First born, this baby I hold in my arms is our first born."

However idyllic it was – or as it now seems to have been – my mind was made up: we would load up a U-Haul trailer, and warmly wrap a three month old baby and head for Kansas City, the headquarters of the Church of the Nazarene, in the middle of winter. What never occurred to me was that I was taking the final step in my move out of the church that had nurtured me in the faith. It seems so ironic that my decision to go to the Nazarene Seminary, instead of continuing at the more liberally oriented Oberlin Seminary, was made to prepare me more adequately for the Nazarene ministry. But, in going there, I became convinced that in all honesty, I could not function with integrity as a Nazarene minister.

Chapter 6

"And he went out, not knowing... ."
Hebrews 11:8

It was a cold January day when I steered the Nash Rambler, with a U Haul trailer attached, out onto route 18 and headed west for Kansas City. I marvel, not only at my courage, if, in fact, courage is what it was, but also at Wave's unwillingness to offer any countervailing opinion about this move. Any resistance she might have offered would have been seen by most clear thinking people as justified.

It is certainly what her parents thought. What must we be thinking – or as they no doubt put it, out of earshot of me, what must he be thinking. Why, Vicky, their first grandchild, wasn't even three months old yet. The pregnancy had not been an easy one, and although I don't remember Wave being concerned over hers being a shortened recuperative period, it had to be of great concern to her parents.

Wave and I did have serious questions about the trip, in the dead of winter, with a small baby. If we had been older and more experienced in all the care an infant demanded, we might have put my seminary plans on hold. I do not recall that either of us spent much time fretting over economic matters. Perhaps we had saved a bit. Whatever we managed to save, could not have been much, and certainly wouldn't last for any extended period of time. Our plan was for me to go to school full time, and Wave would get a teaching position. The teacher shortage made her employment seem a sure thing, and Vicky would be placed in a day care run by the wife of a college friend. Joe Williamson, the college friend who, along with me, had made much sport of Wave's name at the freshman reception at ENC, and remained a very close friend for the rest of those college years, had said we could stay with him and Eleanor until we found an apartment. Since young people tend not to think that far ahead, it seemed to us that we had the basics covered.

Wave now tells me that she did have one concern about this move. She does not share my view that I went to seminary fully convinced that I was going there to prepare to be a Nazarene minister. As she remembers it, she and I were, at the time, discussing the issues I had with the Nazarene Church – its picayune rules about such things as women wearing lipstick and either men or women wearing any kind of jewelry, its belief in sinless perfection – and my questioning whether in fact, given these doubts, I could function as a minister in the Church of the Nazarene. Her disquiet rested on her suspicion that going to seminary meant that I was on my way to making a decision that she was not certain she was prepared to make.

Harrowing is too strong a word to describe the whole trip to Missouri. It is an apt word for parts of it. In 1957, cigarette lighter baby bottle warmers played little or no part in most parents' lives. Maybe Wave remembers how we managed this. What I remember best are Vicky's hunger cries, and the snow that began to fall one evening. Having grown up in southern Delaware where snow was a once or twice a year occurrence, if that, and riding buses and subways in Boston during college, snow tires or chains were expenditures we could avoid. Either would have helped that tiny rambler pull that loaded U Haul up that steep incline somewhere in Illinois. What helped us make it to the other side of the hill was a semi that pulled up behind us and ever so gently nudged car and trailer up to the top and over.

Since this is a faith journey book, a day-by-day recounting of jobs held, apartments lived in, and classes taken during our year and a half in Kansas City would serve no useful purpose. Some bits and pieces from those days, however, seem necessary to justify the second plank of my faith platform which you may remember is that God is faithful, or, as my children remember me stating it: things have a way of working out.

We stayed with Joe and Eleanor Williamson for a week. Vicky's children love to hear that she slept in a dresser drawer – opened – we hasten to add. Our stay in the first apartment was short; the landlady, trying to make ends meet I suppose, kept the thermostat set very low. Wave got a teaching job, and my classes were going well. Being able to go to school full time, for the first time, reconnecting with old college friends, and making new ones – we were content and happy in this new life of ours. A darling daughter, old friends, nice apartment, more money than we had ever had – life was very good.

But just as the trees were beginning to bud, Wave and I had to face the fact that nature wasn't the only thing coming to life. A trip to Dr. Montello confirmed our suspicions: Wave was pregnant. Both of us, resenting his lecture at the time, have quoted him so often ever since. Dr. Montello let us wring our hands a bit – how are we going to possibly manage this coming change in our life; Wave has to work; we moved all the way out here; now this – then he cut us off, and had his say. The first words out of his mouth were how blessed we ought to feel. "Are you aware," he lectured, "how many couples I see who can't have children?"

His last word was an attempt to allay some of our fears. "When they are both out of the diaper stage," he assured us, "the worst will be over, and their thirteen months age difference will prove to be an asset. They will grow up being buddies." We left his office feeling somewhat better, but still not sure how it was all going to work itself out.

It did. Wave was able to continue teaching for the rest of the school year, and with the aid of another college friend – who put in a good word for me with his boss – I got a part time job selling business courses with Draughan's College of Commerce. It was evening work – allowing me to have afternoons for study – and it paid well. Well enough to support us after she stopped teaching.

Wave's fears were justified: my going to the seminary meant my leaving the Nazarene Church. It did not occur there. When I graduated a year and a half later, I took a Nazarene Church to do as my father asked me: give it a year; see how it goes. But it was at the seminary that the psychological wall came down. And I knew it was only a matter of time.

The classes, themselves, helped make up my mind for me. The professors all had been stamped with the holiness imprimatur. If they had any faith doubts, they kept them to themselves. The textbooks, at least the theology texts, were hot off the true believer press. However, instead of confirming the faith I had been raised on, this lock step approach to teaching began to raise serious questions for me.

For instance, I had never read a whole volume of systematic theology, Nazarene style. Seeing, in print, all the claims that were being made for this doctrine of second blessing holiness – no sin, no anger, just joy and bliss here on out – and never having found such a blessing myself, nor seen anyone else who had, I began to wonder. At the time we were reading the holiness texts, we were also reading some of the contemporary theologians. In the late fifties, the prevailing theology was neo-orthodoxy. Neo-orthodoxy, with its war torn European origins, was a reaction to liberalism's rosy optimism. Liberalism preached that the world is getting better and better, and neo-orthodoxy countered, reminding all within earshot that the fruits of that long ago fall in Eden's garden live on – in all of us; even in nature itself.

Some of us – and this brings me to the second major influence in my seminary life – began to ask questions in class about these holiness claims of ours, given what we were reading in the likes of Barth, Brunner and Niehbuhr. Sinless perfection, we would suggest, seems hardly a goal for any of us, given the inherent sinfulness of us all. At least this is what our collateral reading seems to suggest. And what about the Lord's Prayer, we asked one day. Didn't Jesus instruct us when we pray to ask God to forgive us of our sins? Dear Dr. Grider didn't seem ready for that question, and he was a lot brighter than his stupid answer makes him seem. He said, "The Lord's Prayer was never meant to be a private prayer. It should only be prayed in public, where, in all probability, there will be at least one or two sinners present."

The "some of us" who began asking these questions were given a name: we were known as "that group." And we reveled in this notoriety. When the other students would be filing into morning chapel services, we would be heading out for coffee at a nearby restaurant – often making a grand show of it by putting on our coats in plain view of the worshipping faithful. Some afternoons, when we had decided that spending time in a movie theater would be preferable to spending time in the library, we made an equally grand exit from the seminary parking lot. Although viewing a Hollywood production was a sin for the Nazarene Church, we were not about to slink away in silence.

It seems all so adolescent now – this behavior of ours – and it was. But it was necessary. Educators call it differentiation; we group members were separating ourselves from the faith of our fathers and mothers, and beginning the arduous process of fashioning a faith of our own. To say it as the apostle Paul said it, we were "working out our own salvation with fear and trembling."

And there was fear and trembling present in "that group," as well as sadness. We loved the headiness of it all: thumbing our noses at silly church rules; testing wits with our professors; and, with little justification, feeling intellectually superior to our fellow students. We also knew not so deep down beneath all our bravado that the days ahead were not going to be easy.

All of us had grown up in the Nazarene Church, and graduated from Nazarene colleges. This church had not only given us our faith, but many of our friends. All of us talked fondly of some past college professors. Two members of our group had fathers who held the highest position in the Church of the Nazarene, and both fathers had been president of Eastern Nazarene College. Leaving the Nazarene Church would cause serious disruptions in their family life. Although the rest of us did not share this particular burden, we did each of us know that leaving the Nazarene Church meant leaving friends and severing connections with your college.

On an occasional afternoon we would gather in the seminary commons room and talk. One afternoon someone brought along a book written by a Nazarene preacher's daughter. She had left the church years before, and had become an Episcopalian. The book, For Heaven's Sake, is a poignant account of how it had been for her growing up in the Nazarene Church. We began to read this book aloud at our commons room sessions. We would laugh at the hilarious accounts of scary revival sermons she remembered, and the utter embarrassment experienced when the collapsible organ she was not only playing for a street meeting, but also hiding behind, collapsed. We didn't just laugh during these afternoon readings. Some days we cried. And the tears didn't flow from any well of resentment built up over the years as a result of feeling that the Nazarene Church had abused us. The tears I remember are those that came as a result of identifying with Hannah Smith's church experiences – the joys as well as the fears – and identifying with the pain she felt in leaving, and sensing that we would, in all probability, follow her out.

With the exception of Roger Young, we all did. He stayed with the Nazarene Church. His father was one of the high church executives. Maybe that had something to do with his decision. He did not enter the preaching ministry. He chose instead to be a counselor. Joe Williamson, the other son of a Nazarene General Superintendent, became a minister in the United Church of Christ. After receiving a Ph. D. from Harvard, he combined a career of seminary teaching with parish ministry. He just retired from his position as Dean of the Chapel at Princeton. Joe and I have stayed in touch, and Wave and I had dinner with him and his wife, Donna, not long ago. Joe is in the early stages of Alzheimer's – a fate I can't even imagine for one so bright, so quick with the quip, and such an engaging conversationalist. Harry Romeril, the fun loving, also bright, expressive one of the group, entered Princeton's doctoral program after seminary, and died two years later with cancer. Darrell Holland went into journalism and retired a few years ago as religious editor of the Cleveland Plain Dealer. I don't know what happened to Chuck Taylor. He was one of my favorites. When we were loading into a car one afternoon to go see a movie – a first ever experience for me – he said, "Tom, you have never seen anything like these big screens." He was right. I hadn't. "Raintree County" was not a great movie, and

I don't remember Montgomery Clift being awarded an Oscar for his performance in it. But it will always have a place on any list of all time favorites I put together. Don Carpenter wrote me shortly after I became a Methodist, but there was never any contact after that. Our life together as a group was short lived – a mere eighteen months – but it was a time that had life changing consequences for me.

Something else occurred during my Kansas City sojourn that let me know that perhaps the faith of my father's church wasn't a good fit for me: I became a pastor of Orrick Methodist Church.

In the late 1950's, the Methodist Church did not have a seminary anywhere near Kansas City. St. Paul's Seminary would be opened in years to come, but when I was there, the Methodists were looking for part time pastors to fill the pulpits of those small town/country churches in that area. I had tried to get a Nazarene church, but there were not any available. So when I heard that Methodists looked kindly toward these Nazarene boys, I applied and was accepted. My life long dream to be a Methodist was partially fulfilled. I was still a card carrying Nazarene, but finally, Sunday mornings would find me worshipping in a Methodist church.

Orrick was a small railroad town northeast of Kansas City that had seen better days. The church was small as Methodist churches go, but large enough by Nazarene standards. A downside to this appointment was that besides a Sunday morning service, there was also a Sunday evening service as well as a mid-week prayer service. The downside had nothing to do with the three services. This was the pattern in Nazarene circles. It did surprise me a bit when I heard that these "godless" Methodists worshipped every bit as much as the "god-fearing" Nazarenes. My downside concerned workload. What on earth could I find to say in three sermons a week, and when would I ever find the time to put whatever I found worth saying in some kind of preachable form. Still working at the business college and carrying a full load of classes, husband, father of one infant with another on the way, I wondered how I would fit it all in.

We did, and there is nothing royal about the "we." The "we" here includes Wave. Although she no longer worked outside the home, as we later came to say, her days were full with diapers, meals, and typing papers for me. The church found us a small house in Orrick – a delightful place to bring a new baby home to – surrounded by good neighbors and lovingly considerate church members.

The shove out the doors of the Nazarene Church that this little Missouri congregation gave me, was letting me see, first hand, that all I had been taught about the "mainline" denominations – those who were Christian in name only –might be open to question. At least it didn't seem to be true for this particular mainline church. These Orrick Methodists took their faith rather seriously. They smoked cigarettes, and, unless my nose deceived me, some of them drank. They attended movies; I heard them talk about it. God forbid, they played cards. The telephone operator told me so. Orrick's phone system – like those in other rural areas – bordered on the primitive. There were no dials on the phones. To make a call, you would pick up the receiver, give the operator the number you wanted to reach, and she would connect you. One night, when I gave the operator the number for Mildred Larkin, the operator said, "She isn't home tonight. She's over at Mary K. Sandersen's playing bridge." But these card playing, movie going, smoking, drinking Methodists were some of the warmest, kindest, most loving people I had ever met. They met none of the standards I had been taught were necessary if you had any hope at all of receiving second blessing holiness. All they did was exemplify its advertised results. They were faithful in worship. They prayed. They read their Bibles. All things I had been told they did not do. They also appeared anxious to lead richer and fuller lives, or, as we in the trade put it, "to grow in the grace and knowledge of our Lord."

An epiphany of sorts occurred the day I went to the Methodist bookstore in Kansas City, and, took off the shelves a book by an author I not only had never read, but had never even heard his name. It was the title that caught my attention – <u>When the Lamp Flickers</u> – but it was the table of contents that convinced me I should purchase it. The book is a collection of Sunday evening sermons preached by Leslie Weatherhead when he was pastor at the London City Temple. The sermons are his answers to questions submitted by members of his congregation, and before I pulled out of my parking space an hour or so later, I had read about half of them. There, in print, I saw, for the very first time, some of the questions that had been rattling around in my head for years: "Is every word in the Bible true? Is there a Hell? Is there an unpardonable sin?"

That Kansas City street was my Damascus Road equivalent. I didn't see Paul's blinding light that day, but something like his "scales" did fall from my eyes, and the answers Leslie Weatherhead gave to his congregation, and was now giving to me, were answers I could give, with integrity, to the congregations I would one day serve.

The Orrick church liked me every bit as much as I liked them. They begged me to stay, all the while knowing that with Tommy's birth in November, their part time salary couldn't possibly cover the expenses of a family of four. Maureen Offutt, church organist and teacher in the Orrick School, tried to use her influence to secure a teaching position for me. I could teach, the school said, they would love to have me; but I would first have to take some education courses to get certified. That did not appeal to me. I had gone to school to prepare for the parish ministry. I wanted no more schooling. I was ready for a full time church of my own.

Besides, I felt I should honor my Dad's wishes. The least I could do for him was to give the Nazarene Church – the one that had brought new life to him and his family – a year. He was also very sick, and although no one thought his death was imminent, those who were closest to him, felt that he had only a few years left, at best. The church available that was nearest my Delaware home was in Easton, Maryland – just twenty miles away.

Neither Wave nor I recall the trip from Missouri, suggesting to us that the move was without incident. Traveling in early June meant no icy roads to negotiate, and Tommy and Vicky were both well past that three month infant stage that, along with the snow and ice, had made the earlier trip that much more difficult.

What seems particularly strange is that I do not remember my last Sunday as pastor of Orrick Church. I remember every final sermon at every church I have served since, but not there. One would think I would. This was my first congregation. It was where I conducted my very first funeral. In my minds eye, I can see the funeral parlor in nearby Richmond, Missouri. I can also picture the gravesite, situated on a bit of a slope, which was to be Bessie Campbell's final resting place. It was a windy winter day, with a slight, misty rain falling, and my shivering lips and chattering teeth – the result of both my anxiety and my thinking that a thin plastic raincoat could double as a lined topcoat – made mouthing the words of committal extremely difficult. I didn't shiver a few months later when I married Sam and Maureen Offutt's oldest son. I just trembled. It was my very first wedding, and this time my anxiety expressed itself in shaky hands, weak knees and profuse sweating.

Orrick Church will always be special for me. They gave me an engraved Shaeffer "Snorkel" fountain pen, which I still use, thanks to the overhauling the Fountain Pen Hospital in New York City gave it a few years back. One of the church's commemorative plates hangs in a prominent spot on our sunroom wall. Most of those wonderful people who opened their hearts and their lives to this twenty-five year old kid and tacked "Reverend" on to his name have gone on to be with Bessie Campbell. Maureen Offutt, that first "mainline" saint I was privileged to meet, kept in touch until she died a few years back at the age of 92. She told me from the start that I was a gifted preacher. What she meant – what I took her to mean, any way – was that she saw in my early on struggling to put this faith of ours into words, certain gifts that age and experience could possibly develop. I was in Kansas City on business a few years back, rented a car, and drove to Orrick. I knew that after Sam died, she sold the farm, and had moved into town. Since everyone in that small town knew Maureen, it was easy to get directions. We had such fun recalling those few months I was there, yet, for her and for me, a significant time. What I treasure from that last conversation with her is hearing her say that she never sings the hymn, "Great is Thy Faithfulness," without thinking of me. She says I used to sing it as a solo when I was there. I don't remember doing that. I'm glad I did, though, simply because what it means is that early on in my preaching life I was at least faintly aware that God's faithfulness – we will get what we need – ought to be a part of any faith story I planned to tell.

The Orrick commemorative plate and my snorkel pen, along with a few snapshots, are the only memorabilia we have from our time in Missouri. Our son Tommy's birth certificate listing Research Hospital in Kansas City as his place of birth could also be classed as a bit of memorabilia from those long ago days. Our only living connection with Orrick is the Christmas card we get each year from Eldon Woods, the town postmaster when we were there, and his wife, Marilyn. Plates and pens aside, what I carry around with me is the firm conviction that I am a Methodist preacher today because I spent a few months in the presence of some saints who lived in a little railroad town in western Missouri, and helped me start to put together a faith that I could honestly claim as my own, and preach with integrity.

Chapter 7

"Once to every man and nation, comes the moment to decide... ."
James Russell Lowell

Although the decision to give the Nazarene Church a year's trial had been my father's idea, I found myself looking forward to the move back east. It would be good to be close to my family – especially my Dad. It had been ten months since my last visit, and from the reports I was receiving from home his health was deteriorating rapidly. Another thing that made this move an anticipated one, was the thought of being a full time pastor – with my own church.

The Easton, Maryland, Church of the Nazarene was what the denomination referred to as a "home mission." A home mission was defined as a new church – usually in a growing community – that would have to receive denominational support in its start-up phase. Then, after a hoped for short period of growth, the congregation would assume all its operational expenses. What this meant for me is that the Washington/Philadelphia District would pay my forty-five dollar a week salary and provide me with a place to live.

The church had been organized about five years prior to my coming, but had still not reached the self-supporting stage. The organizing pastor, ironically, was the "church-builder" type who, along with my father, had constructed the Seaford Church of the Nazarene. Brother Bailey found a choice corner lot in the expanding section of Easton, and constructed a house/church that would become the parsonage when the congregation grew enough to support the construction of a church building. The woman pastor who followed Brother Bailey, stayed for a very short time and left, rather abruptly, in the middle of the night.

The house/church scheme was a bit of a comedown, though not unexpected. In quartet travels during my college summers, I had sung in Nazarene Churches of all shapes and sizes: storefronts, basements, even a barn that, at one time, had painted on one of its sides, "Choose Mail Pouch Tobacco – Treat Yourself to the Best" – an advertisement that painting and aging had not been able to erase. Knowing this, I did not expect an Orrick Methodist equivalent: stained glass windows, dark oak pews, and a pipe organ. But as Nazarene Churches went in those days, Easton Church's "great room" was attractive and, for a non-liturgical church, even worshipful.

There were just eighteen full members on the church rolls. Attendance at worship however, numbered about forty. You see, to be a full member in the Church of the Nazarene, one had to meet its rather strict requirements: no smoking, no drinking, no card playing, and no movies. This meant – and, perhaps, still does mean – that Sunday school and worship attendance exceeded church membership in most Nazarene churches.

A troubling fact was that six of the church's eighteen members were from the same family, and since holding office in a local church was limited to full church members, this one family sat in most of the seats of power. Even more troubling for me was that this family – in particular its matriarch – was long on what I had come to view as non-essentials, and short on what I had come to see as essentials.

For instance, grand-mom, made much of the church's recommended dress code for those who made any claim at all to living the holy life. The Manual (the Nazarene Church's official book of discipline) specifically stated that Christians, Nazarene style, should not "adorn themselves" with either "gold or costly apparel." People should dress modestly at all times – especially women. Grand-mom and daughter did exactly that. Both of them wore dresses that covered them from their necks to all four of their extremities. They wore no jewelry, and their hair was wrapped tightly in buns. To them they were not only obeying the "Manual", but also the divine word of God. To me, though, it soon became apparent that they were skipping over some of God's other words – especially those best delivered by his son, Jesus: words about love, kindness and forgiveness; and especially the word or two about withholding judgment and leaving that up to the One who alone is fit to judge. Mama and daughter both had sharp tongues, and were all too ready to come to God's assistance in the matter of separating the sheep from the goats.

Had this family been the heart and soul of the Easton church, I could not have lasted the year. They weren't. Among the other twelve members were some delightful people. They made no boast of having attained any sort of Christian perfection, and although the women followed the church's dress code of no make-up and no jewelry, their dresses pretty much followed the fashion of the day.

Enough new people began to come, that there were times I thought I might be able to make a go of being a Nazarene pastor. With two babies at home, I took over a corner of the church for an office. Scheduling my days like Paul Baxter had taught me, I read and wrote every morning and called on members and visitors every afternoon. Someone told me that Harry Emerson Fosdick, famed minister at Riverside Church in New York City, spent an hour in preparation for every minute he would spend in the pulpit. So I began the life long practice of writing out my sermons. Years later when I served a church of 2500 members, I loved to remind that congregation that I spent the same amount of time preparing sermons for my first church of 18 members that I did for them.

The church grew that first summer, helped along by an all neighborhood push for our vacation Bible school. A few of us canvassed the neighborhood, handing out prizes, and the children came. Soon they started showing up for Sunday school and for church. Before long there were a hundred people sitting out in front of me on Sunday mornings.

Wave and I loved the town of Easton. There was at that time a cultural sophistication about it that set it apart from other Eastern Shore towns. The country club gave ministers free memberships, and a doctor I met on the golf course invited me to join the Kiwanis Club. I became active in the local clergy association, participating in ecumenical worship services, and joining in other religious community ventures.

At the same time, I did my duty not only to my local church but also to my denominational district. I volunteered to serve as a counselor at our boys and girls camp. I renewed acquaintances with some college friends who were now pastors on the Washington/Philadelphia District, and also some of the pastors I had met in my quartet traveling days. The District Superintendent praised me for my work in finally getting this mission church moving in the right direction. Easton Church was growing, and much of the credit for this was being given to me.

However, I knew that the time for decision had come. It was not possible for me to continue living in two church worlds, which is what I was doing. Being on the golf course, eating lunch at Kiwanis meetings, or sitting around tables at ecumenical gatherings, made me aware of that whole other non-Nazarene world that existed out there – the same non-Nazarene faith world that I had experienced at Orrick. And I realized that the psychological wall that had started tumbling in Orrick was now down for good; in my honest moments, I knew that I did not belong in the Nazarene world.

The emphasis they placed on trivial issues, such as movies, dancing, and card playing, to the neglect of having anything to say about peace, or justice, or equality of opportunity, struck me as skewed thinking from people who spent so much time talking about "perfect love." My differences began to show. I could never preach against these "trivial issues", and in those pre-lung cancer/cigarette smoking days, I didn't even preach against the sinfulness of lighting up. I did try to put my spin on what John Wesley might have had in mind when he talked about "going on to perfection", and, in all honesty, I did use a few of the Nazarene's holiness buzz words. But, to liberally paraphrase scripture, people know when the trumpet they are hearing is giving off an uncertain sound.

So I started being asked what I thought about these rules that kept these non-Nazarene-world types from becoming full church members. They had never heard me preach against smoking, drinking, and the movies, so now, all of a sudden, what's the big deal? Their beginning to ask me, "What do you think, Tom?" made it a personal integrity issue. I was being paid forty-five dollars a week and given a house to live in to establish a Nazarene Church. And given where my head and heart were, not only was I not doing that, the truth was that I couldn't do that.

A few weeks before my Dad died, we had all gathered for Sunday dinner at the house in Bethel. For those who stayed close to home – which was everyone except Luther and me – Sunday dinners at home were command performances. I preached at Easton, then Wave and I loaded up

Vicky and Tommy and we joined the rest of the family around the table. Everyone didn't come – the dining room wasn't that large – and I don't remember which sisters and husbands were present. Sometime early on in the meal, I made some negative comment about either the Nazarene Church in general or the Easton Nazarene Church in particular. My father, seated at the head of the table, clothes hanging loosely on his skin and bones body, turned an icy stare in Wave's direction and said, "This is all your doing. If you hadn't come along, he never would have thought this way." Wave got up from the table, and ran crying to an upstairs bedroom. Daddy's mumbled, quasi apology, was, "Well, I guess I messed things up." The best "you go straight to hell" I could muster in those pre-therapy days, was, "You've got it all wrong, Daddy. I'm the one who has a problem with the church."

Wave came back to the table, we finished eating, and a few weeks later my Dad made his passage over to the other side. We never discussed the church again.

In a previous chapter I told about my father's death and funeral service. What I did not tell then is what Luther, Harley Bye, the pastor who conducted his memorial service, and I did in the evening following his burial in the afternoon. We went to the movies.

The pastor was a college friend. He and his wife were both classmates of Wave and me. He was not on his way out of the church at that time, although years later he was summarily dismissed because of his "liberal" views, which, I suppose were beginning to bud when he went with Luther and me to see "No Time for Sergeants." We laughed our "fool heads off" – a Mama phrase – and I do not recall feeling any remorse over doing so; neither do I recall telling any of the rest of the family what Luther and I had done.

Since leaving Kansas City and assuming my role as a Nazarene pastor, Wave and I had not seen any movies. Perhaps this trip to one of "Satan's Hell Holes" – as I had heard local movie houses referred to – was a thumbing of my nose in the direction of that towering figure that for so many years had stood, like an un-parted Red Sea, between me and that mainline church Promised Land. If that was my intent – and some later fifty-minute hours spent on a therapist's couch strongly suggested that it was – it didn't register with me at the time.

My father's death did, however, set the exit wheels in motion. My sister Jane had been working for a few years as the secretary for a local Methodist minister. He was a dearly loved pastor, and had been at the Mt. Olivet Church in Seaford for seventeen years. His wife struggled with a bi-polar disorder, although we had no name for it then. His son was confined to a mental hospital suffering from schizophrenia. I tell this because these crosses that Walter Stone carried made his an empathic ear. He was seen as a wise and compassionate counselor – a well-earned reputation.

He made time for me. He listened as I went down my list of grievances with the Nazarene Church. It was not news to him, since my sister Jane, still living in Daddy's physical as well as emotional shadow, had often unburdened her Nazarene trapped soul to him. Walter Stone did not assume the role of a Rogerian therapist. His responses were anything but the grunts and nods, or the "I think I hear you sayings," of those who specialized in the non-directive therapeutic method. This short, bald, Brother Sebastian type weighed in heavily on the side of taking action. It was clear, he felt, that I would be more at home in the Methodist Church. He was positive that I would never be happy in a church that majored on prohibitions, and felt that faith and doubt could never live together under the same soul's roof.

One day in the middle of my mucking around in the same old stuff, he took advantage of a conversational pause, and picked up the phone. "Hi, Leas," he said. "I have a young man here who pastors the Nazarene Church in Easton. He thinks he would like to be a Methodist preacher. Would you talk with him?" After he finished the call, he said to me, "That was Dr. Leas Green, I was talking to. He's the Methodist District Superintendent of the Easton District. He said he would be happy to talk with you about a church."

A few days later, Dr. Green, a distinguished looking sixty-something, a foot taller than Walter Stone, invited me into his study. What was not observable by me when he met me at the door, but soon became apparent when he cut me off mid sentence, was his bottom line business approach. If I were serious about becoming a Methodist preacher, he had a church for me. All I needed to do was say the word. Actually, there were four churches on what Methodism calls a circuit. I would be the pastor of those churches that were in and around a little eastern shore community called Secretary. I thanked him and said I would talk it over with Wave.

She and I located Secretary on a Maryland map and drove out to take a look. The churches were small, and peering through the windows of one of them, we spotted a pot-bellied stove, which immediately dredged up memories for me of all those tiny little out-of-the-way Nazarene churches that I had sung God's praises in for three college summers. Orrick Methodist with the stained glass windows, oak pews and organ, Secretary was not.

Secretary's four churches with its pot-bellied stove was not the only reason I called Dr. Green and refused his offer. Years later, hearing him referred to as a "bull dog," helped explain his "I thought you wanted a church" response to my call telling him I wasn't ready to make the move. I really wasn't ready.

I was so conflicted. After preaching on Sunday mornings, I would put an LP of Tennessee Ernie Ford singing hymns on our pre-stereo Hi-Fi, then stretch out on the couch for my Sunday afternoon post-church nap. As all those old songs I had grown up singing – often with Mama, or my sister Elizabeth playing the piano – touched soul-deep spots within me, leaving this church that was so much a part of me and my faith seemed out of the question. But, the music would go with me, I told myself. Orrick church had taught me that Methodists sing these same hymns – maybe not all of them, but most of them, anyway.

What wasn't so easy for me to dismiss was my concern about losing college friendships. The Nazarene Church was a closely-knit community – a community that included its colleges. To leave the church meant leaving its colleges, especially the one that had meant so much to me. There were the minister friends I had made after college. Most of these were older – one or two were mentors of mine – and looked on me as a rising young star in the Nazarene hierarchy. And my District Superintendent, Doctor Grosse, had known my family for years.

Equally troubling were those new people who had started attending Easton Nazarene Church. They were not your hard core "true believers," and I wondered what effect my leaving might have on them. I was especially concerned for the young people. Wave and I were counselors for the growing youth group. Still in our twenties, we were just adult enough to be looked up to, but not adult enough to remove us from the young people's perceived real world. I also felt that these kids saw in me something approaching a real human being.

This war "in my members," as the Apostle Paul put it, raged on for most of the fall and early winter. Sometime after the first of the year, though in all honesty this is a guess, based on my need to include certain events that I know happened, I began the process to become a Methodist minister.

The first step in the process was a trip back to Walter Stone's office. I asked him to give me the names of some District Superintendents in the neighboring Baltimore Conference of the Methodist Church. Eastern shore Methodists were a part of the Peninsula Conference. The conference is Methodism's diocese or presbytery equivalent. The Baltimore Conference encompassed the District of Columbia, the state of Maryland west of the Chesapeake Bay, and the panhandle of West Virginia. My requesting Baltimore Conference contacts was the result of having been told that, in all probability, I would have to take some seminary courses in Methodist Doctrine and Polity to meet the church's requirements for ordination. Since the closest seminary was Wesley, which had just moved from western Maryland to its new location in Washington, D.C., a move to the Washington area made sense.

Walter gave me a list of the superintendents. He thought a great deal of Paul Warner – they had been in school together – and I picked out two others from the list – choices made for the soundest of reasons: I liked their names. So Daniel Justice and Orris Robinson, along with Paul Warner made up my short list of Methodist contacts.

Not too long after my requests for admission to the Methodist ministry were put in the mail, my brother, Luther, now an assistant pastor in a Nazarene Church in Illinois, and Joyce, his wife, made a visit home to see Mama. They had not been home since Daddy's funeral. Luther agreed to preach for me at Easton church's Sunday evening service. After the service, I rode back to Seaford with them, and spent the night with Mama in the apartment she now rented having sold the house in Bethel.

At some point in the service, I began to develop sharp pains in my stomach. These were not new symptoms with me. Once on a quartet trip in Vermont, I was hospitalized overnight. The doctor there was certain this was appendicitis, although the other classic indications – high blood count, fever, nausea – were not present. He was reluctant to release me, and his parting words were a suggestion that I not plan any ocean liner trips to Europe. Meaning, I guess, that it would be in my best interests to never be too far removed from adequate health care. A couple years later, I spent another hospital overnight for tests, thinking that the severe stomach cramps indicated an ulcer.

Every bounce at every railroad crossing between Easton and Seaford was agony. Luther and Joyce stayed two streets over with my sister Ruth and her family. I stayed in the apartment and slept in Daddy's empty bed. Although, as it later turned out to be the worst thing she could have done, it made sense to my mother to put a hot water bottle on my aching middle. She also felt it would help me sleep if I took one of Daddy's leftover sleeping pills.

I didn't sleep well, and the next morning Dr. Moyer, the family doctor for all our lower Delaware years, made a house call. Of course he didn't say this, but I am convinced that he was certain that this nervous kid he had seen grow up, raised by a mother whose panic attacks were legendary, was suffering from a perforated ulcer. He had me admitted to the hospital, and I was put in a room next to the room where my Dad had died.

Wave had not made the trip to Mama's with me. Not only did she have the care of Vicky and Tommy, she was also finishing out the year for a teacher at Easton Senior High School. She came that evening, and was concerned at how ill I looked. My day had been filled with tests – all seeking to determine the location of this presumed ulcer. I was still in pain and my temperature was climbing. There were more tests on Tuesday, and when Wave came that evening she felt that something needed to be done. It was obvious to her that I was really sick. Early on in our courtship, she learned of my tendencies to hypochondria. It didn't take her long to know that with me, like it had been with my mother, every chest pain was a heart attack and every headache a brain tumor. Wave did get a chance to see the real thing with me, though, when I had my first ever kidney stone attack. That kidney stone pain look was what she saw in my face now.

When she stretched her full five feet one inch frame to its maximum height, and told the doctor in her best award winning debate voice that she had two babies at home, and that she knew their daddy and her husband was really sick, and it was time to do something about it, he agreed and they began to prep me for surgery.

All the family gathered in the lobby of that little hospital where just a few months before Daddy had died. Wave noticed that Luther was exceptionally agitated. He kept walking back and forth, round and round, sitting down and then getting up again to continue his pacing. The surgeon who would assist came by in a tuxedo. He had been called in from a party at the nearby country club. No word. Then, rushing in from the outside – also in a tuxedo – was Dr. Moyer, who said as he rushed by, "It's going to be all right."

Well, no one had thought it wouldn't be – at least not consciously. Maybe at some sub-conscious filial level this was what was driving Luther's emotional engine. Wave was just happy that finally they were taking a look inside me to see what was going on. Now they were worried.

They waited some more. Finally, Dr. Moyer emerged from the surgery unit and said, "It's going to be all right." And this time, his same words seemed more fact than promise. He told Wave, "It was touch and go there for a while, but he's going to be okay."

The touch and go was the result of my appendix having ruptured. The reason I did not have the tell tale signs that could have confirmed appendicitis is that my appendix was in the wrong place. Its unorthodox position kept it from affecting the blood count, confirming the suspicions of the doctor in that Vermont hospital years ago. I wondered about the tube in my side when I awoke, and thought it a bit strange that for two days running they took my blood pressure every half hour. It also seemed out of the ordinary that I was in the hospital for a couple days short of two weeks.

It really was more touch and go than any of us knew, as I found out some weeks later. My sister Ruth worked as a volunteer in the hospital. She was arranging some magazines, and standing near her were two doctors, one of whom had been one of the surgeons who operated on me. This was pre-patient privacy days, so they were discussing quite openly a case involving the death of a twenty-seven year old woman that had occurred during a rather routine varicose vein operation. Ruth overheard Dr. Cooper, the surgeon who assisted in my appendectomy, say, "It reminds me of that twenty-seven year old preacher we had some months back, whom we almost lost on the table."

Rumbling around in Wave's head during this time were not just thoughts about what she would do if something were to happen to me, or how on earth she would explain this to our babies, but there was no doubt in her mind that this would put an end to any of my plans to jump ship on the Nazarenes. Given my "good news of hell" upbringing, surely I would see this as a God shot across my bow.

Fear of any sort of Divine retribution never crossed my mind. My father's wishes were no longer any concern of mine, even though I was in a bed only a few feet away from the bed where he took his last breath. Near the end of my hospital stay, Paul Warner, one of my Methodist district superintendent contacts, called and said he had a church for me. Since the church he offered was in western Maryland – further from the seminary in Washington, D. C. than I wanted to be – I requested some time to think it over. The time requested would also give the Washington superintendent a chance to respond.

Dr. Robinson did call shortly after my release from the hospital. He said he would like to meet me and talk over some of the details involved in a denominational transfer. I agreed and he suggested we meet at Wesley Seminary. I was thrilled. Not only did it seem I was well on my way to becoming a Methodist preacher, this would also give me a chance to check out the new Wesley Seminary.

What never occurred to me was that the appointment date we set would still be in my no driving recuperative period. Wave couldn't take me; she had a class to teach. The adults in the church were also working. The intention of the trip had to be a secret. I did not want to show my hand until I had some guarantee of a job. I do not remember why I placed my job security in the hands of one of the young men in the church. Maybe I had determined that he was the kind who didn't ask questions. I don't really know. However, he agreed to be my driver, and my cover story was that I had to pick up some materials from the seminary library.

If he ever had any questions, he kept them to himself. God knows he had every reason to wonder. When we arrived at the seminary, I took him, whose name I no longer remember, to the library periodical room, and told him I had an appointment, and would come back to the library, pick up the materials I needed, and then we would return home. A good plan, I thought. The only problem was when I entered the room for my interview with Dr. Robinson, he didn't offer me a chair. Rather, after greeting me, he said he would have to go. There was a groundbreaking ceremony for the new Sibley Hospital, and he had been asked to participate in the service. It shouldn't take long, and he would really like to talk to me. Would it be possible for me to wait around? Better still, why didn't I come along to the ceremony? The Bishop would be there as well as members of Congress. Not having any idea how I would explain all this to my driver, I said I would be delighted to come along.

I have no idea what my young Nazarene driver thought about our sitting in a vacant lot on folding chairs, reading prayers (a practice unheard of in the Nazarene tradition), responding to rituals being led by a clerically collared prelate, and singing strange hymns. He and I never discussed it.

It was a trip worth making, although it took a while for me to realize it. What I did not understand at the time, and came to realize only when I became a district superintendent years later, is that, in Methodism, the appointment process works from the top down. And an appointment for a person coming into the Methodist ministry was, of necessity, at or near the bottom of any superintendent's list of placement priorities.

In early May, the Washington/Philadelphia District held its District Assembly. This annual gathering was a combination business and camp meeting. The voting delegates consisted of pastors and elected laypersons from each congregation on the district. Two agenda items concerned me. One was the pastor's report. Each pastor was required to stand before the assembly – presided over by one of the five general superintendents – and give brief highlights of the year's activities in his or her church. It was also a chance to vet the preacher's moral suitability to hold the pastoral office. It functioned a bit like the "if any one can show cause why this couple" phrase in most marriage ceremonies. After each pastor reported, the presiding general superintendent would pause, allowing time for anyone to show just cause, and then he would say, "report received and character passed." My other concern was the review I would be given by the district's Board of Orders and Relations. This was the board that would determine not just my fitness to be a minister in the church universal, but a minister in the Church of the Nazarene as well.

My report time passed without incident. I did work up a bit of a sweat listening to all the reports that preceded mine. They all seemed to contain spirit filled recounts of Holy Ghost revivals held, and listed, in precise detail, how many souls had received not just the first blessing but the second one as well. I had no such outpouring of the spirit to report, so I reported on my record setting vacation Bible school, and my record setting Sunday School and worship attendance numbers, knowing that however much Nazarenes talked about the "winds of the spirit blowing where they will," they really liked to count heads. When I had finished, and the silence that followed was uninterrupted by anyone showing cause why I should not be granted the denomination's ministerial seal of approval, the General Superintendent broke the silence with a gaveled comment, "report received and character passed."

As I had thought just might be the case, the Board of Orders and Relations posed the bigger hurdle. And I was prepared. Buoyed with a measure of confidence that the Methodists wanted me, I was ready to spread out before these elders in the church the doctrinal issues about which I had major questions: chief among them being the whole matter of "Christian perfection," or, as they liked to put it, "second blessing holiness."

There were approximately thirty fully ordained elders facing me as I took my seat beside the chair of the board in the front of a conference room in the educational wing of the First Church of the Nazarene in Baltimore, Maryland. There was probably a prayer offered, and maybe a word of greeting to me, although I don't remember either of those things occurring. The first words I remember being said to me were, "Tom, we understand that your wife wears make-up."

I couldn't believe it. At some level, I did know that these "trivial issues" were of grave concern to segments of the church. But I expected more from a clergy board whose sole responsibility was to pass judgment on a candidate's fitness for ministry. My reputation had preceded me – being a member of "that group" at seminary – I knew that. So it seemed logical to me that they would want to hear from me, directly, what I thought about some of the cardinal doctrines of the church. Certainly, I imagined, they would want to know if I thought I could function as a pastor in the Church of the Nazarene holding, as they had heard I held, serious questions about the possibility of any human being attaining such a state of sinless perfection. But what I thought about heart holiness was not high on their list of priorities. What I thought about my wife wearing "makeup" was.

I smiled and said, "Yes, she does." "How much," someone else asked. Then I laughed when I said, "I have no idea 'how much.' She doesn't paint herself up like a Jezebel, if that's what you mean. She uses a bit of rouge and some lipstick." After a few more salvos about what my wife put on her face, they turned their attention to me.

Again, I was dumbfounded. Their first question about me, the applicant, was about my wedding band. An overweight preacher, dressed to the nines, with a crisply starched shirt and a well-cut suit, introduced his question with a comment. "I see you are wearing a wedding ring." He then asked if I were aware of the "Manual's" prohibition against "adorning ourselves with gold and costly apparel." If there was a single moment of decision for me – an exact time that I knew I couldn't remain a Nazarene – this was the moment. Knowing that I had Methodist offers – at least the promise of offers – I gave myself an "oh, what the hell" permission to speak my mind. So I looked my questioner in the eye, and said, "Yes, I am aware of the Manual's statement about wearing gold. What strikes me as interesting, though, is that there is more gold in your cuff links and tie bar than there is in my simple wedding band." The rest of that hour and a half is a blur. I wish it had been taped.

I remember well what followed. Dr. Gross, my district superintendent, was present in the meeting, and he never opened his mouth. When I was excused so that the board might vote on my suitability for the Nazarene ministry, he excused himself. When we got out in the hall, he put his arm around me and apologized for the grilling I had received. I then said to him, "Dr. Grosse, what upsets me most is that I went into that meeting fully prepared to lay my theological cards on the table. I was ready to spell it all out: my beliefs and how that might not make me a suitable candidate for ministry in the Nazarene Church. But they didn't seem to care about any of that. For all they know, I may not even believe in God." Since all I was asking for was to be licensed as a preacher, I passed the Board's review. If the bar had been raised to the suitability for ordination, I have no doubt the decision of the board would not have been the same.

In just a few weeks, Dr. Robinson phoned and said he had two churches for me. It was my call. One was in a small Chesapeake Bay town named Shadyside. The other was a circuit of two churches on Capitol Hill in southeast Washington. Which one did I want? When I told him that I knew nothing about either, he made the choice for me. Given the fact that we had two small children, Shadyside, or so it seemed to him, would be the best place for us. And just like we had done with the offer of churches in Secretary, Maryland, Wave and I made a trip to Shadyside. Only this time, we fell in love with the offer. The church occupied a prominent spot in the town, and it did seem like a comfortable place for our family.

I informed Dr. Grosse of my decision and he requested that I not tell the congregation my real reason for leaving. My cover story was that I was going back to school, which, of course was true. I invited him to preach at Easton a few weeks before my final Sunday. We also invited him to dinner after the service. Seated in the living room after the meal, with three year old Vicky and two year old Tommy making their pre-nap presence felt, he asked, in all sincerity, "Tom, have you considered your children's eternal welfare?" Just in case that needs translating, in Dr. Grosse's Nazarene world view, my joining the Methodist Church meant that I was positioning myself, and my precious children, on a slippery slope that would lead straight to Hell. And his was one of the church's moderate voices. An item on my "to do" list that never got scratched off was a letter to Dr. Grosse. I wanted to thank him for the support he had been to me, and also to tell him that those two toddlers whose eternal destiny he had been so concerned about had somehow managed to find their way in the Methodist Church. Vicky stayed close enough to God to hear him calling her into the ministry of the church, and Tommy, who also kept the faith, now uses his legal skills to serve not only his Methodist denomination, but other church groups as well. The last time I sat down to write the letter, word came that Dr. Grosse had died. What I then did was send an email to one of his sons – a college friend of mine – telling him what I had intended to tell his Dad. Easton Church bought me a new suit as a farewell present, which I wore to my first ever session of a Methodist Annual Conference.

Chapter 8

"We Methodists think and let think."
John Wesley

Finally, the time had come for me to cross over into the "Promised Land" of Methodism. All those days, for all those years, staring at all those forms with the blank asking for my church affiliation waiting to be filled, and wishing more than anything else, that I could fill it with Methodist instead of Nazarene. I was almost there.

First, though, I had to be accepted by the Methodists. Their equivalent to the Nazarene's Board of Orders and Relations would want to interview me, I was told, and the entire Baltimore Conference Session would have to vote to accept me. This should not be a major concern, Walter Stone said as he tried to assure me that I would have no problem. Hadn't I already been offered a church? And, wasn't it true that the Methodist Church was experiencing a shortage of preachers.

The day before I left for Western Maryland College in Westminster, Maryland, the site of the Baltimore Conference session, Dr. Robinson called to tell me that Shadyside would not be the place where I would begin my life as a Methodist preacher. My first layover in Methodism's

"Promised Land," he told me, would be on Capitol Hill in Southeast Washington, D.C. He gave no reason for the change in plans, and I asked for none. Years later, the minister who had gone to Shady Side instead of me explained it all. He had been in the conference for a few years, which meant he had seniority in appointment matters. He had served an inner city church in Baltimore, and, as he put it, had "paid his dues." So, when they called to tell him his appointment was in southeast Washington, he told them that he was through with inner city churches, and wanting them to fully understand the depth of his displeasure at their offer, he told them what they could do with it. Literally. Known for his salty tongue, it did not surprise his district superintendent to be told that he could take that Capitol Hill appointment and "shove it up his ass." Two reasons I am glad I was not given these details at the time: I was not ready to learn that preachers, even liberal Methodist preachers, said such things; I was also not ready to learn how low I was on Methodism's appointment priority list.

Nothing could dampen my excitement at heading off for my first annual conference session. What made it doubly sweet is that my brother Luther made the trip with me. His year as an associate in his father-in-law's church had convinced him, as my year in Easton had convinced me, that he could not, with integrity, function as a pastor in the Nazarene Church. Luther was given a student appointment so that he could enter Wesley Seminary. His first Methodist Church assignment was a two-point circuit in a lovely northern Maryland community. Luther not only brought his wife of one year, Joyce, into Methodism, but her mother and father as well. Joyce's father, Dr. C.B. Strang, was a prominent minister in the Nazarene Church. He had served two of the denominations largest churches, been a member of the Nazarene Church's prestigious General Board, and seriously considered for the presidency of the Nazarene Church's one and only seminary. But at the age of sixty-five, he, too, admitted that he was, at heart, not one of the Nazarene Church's "true believers."

The three of us escapees from the Nazarene Church caused quite a stir at the conference session. Westminster's local newspaper did a story on us. We had immediate name recognition, which, to be honest, stood all three of us in good stead in the years to come. For some reason, not just a few thought Dr. Strang was our father, and for years, even after he moved to Florida to start a church at age seventy in Vero Beach, I would be asked how my Dad was doing. After a while, I stopped trying to clear it up, and gave whatever the latest news I had on Dr. Strang to my questioner.

The conference session was more than I had ever dreamed it would be. The Bishop of the Washington area, G. Bromley Oxnam, was out of the country, and another bishop was presiding. It was a bit of a disappointment, since I was anxious to see this rather famous churchman. He, along with Edward R. Murrow, was given a great deal of credit for ending Senator Joseph McCarthy's reign of terror. Bishop Oxnam's name appeared on McCarthy's list of clergy who "served God on Sunday and the Communist Party the rest of the week." The Bishop would have none of it and demanded a hearing before the House Un-American Activities Committee where his brilliant mind and meticulous record keeping tied the Senator and his committee in knots.

The fill-in Bishop for that 1959 session of the Baltimore Annual Conference was named, of all things, John Wesley Lord. What other career path could he have possibly chosen, Luther and I wondered. If John Wesley Hardin's last name had been Lord, perhaps he could have avoided living a life of crime. Luther and I sat in the balcony of the college's Alumni Hall and watched in amazement as the conference proceeded. Elections were in progress for delegates to the upcoming General Conference the following year. The ballot results were listed on a chalkboard positioned on the stage behind the bishop. Asbury Smith was the frontrunner, followed closely by Norman Trott, Cranston Riggin, Clarence Fossett, Orris Robinson; all persons who would come to play important roles in Luther's life and in mine. There were spirited discussions in the sessions on war and peace, hunger, and other issues that were referred to as "social concerns." Delegates were constantly rushing to microphones to debate the pros and cons of this resolution or that to be sent off challenging something the government was or was not doing.

The "sin of racial segregation" seemed to be on everyone's mind. Especially at the session when four well dressed black men were ushered on to the platform and seated off to the left of the presiding officer, Bishop Lord. When they were introduced as "fraternal delegates" from the Washington Conference, I had no idea what that meant. What I came to know was that in June 1959, not only was society segregated, so was the Methodist Church. In the middle of the 19th century, the Methodist Church, like some other denominations, split over the issue of slavery. Then in 1939, the desire for church unity trumped church conscience, and the pro-slavery Methodist Church South agreed to a re-union that institutionalized segregation in the church. The plan of union stipulated that the Methodist Church would be divided into jurisdictions. Five of them would be geographically configured, and one racially. This meant that all the black Methodist Churches in the denomination would be a part of the Central Jurisdiction. The four "fraternal delegates" seated on the platform in front of me were from near by churches in the cities of Baltimore and Washington. Because of the color of their skin, however, they were from another jurisdiction.

Bits and pieces of this history I picked up that day in the debate that followed the fraternal delegates' introduction. A resolution was introduced to recommend to the upcoming General Conference that the Central Jurisdiction be abolished. I remember one impassioned speaker, with a decidedly southern drawl, likening such action to a reneging on one's wedding vows. His was a lone voice. The resolution passed.

This was my promised land, flowing with its version of milk and honey. Nobody mentioned movies, or dancing, or card playing. Earrings dangled from women's ears and every preacher I spotted wore a wedding band. There was some talk of the evils of drinking, though. Rumor had it that beer was readily available for students at American University in Washington, D. C., one of Methodism's secondary schools. But, this was as close as the conference session came to any of the trivial pursuits that had been so much a part of my Nazarene days.

What also made it such a wonderful time is how much a lot of it resembled Northeast Camp – without the "hell-fire" preaching. I loved those August weeks at camp, in spite of its Jonathan Edwards' "Sinners in the Hands of an Angry God" type sermons. I especially loved the tabernacle full of people singing the hymns that were so much a part of me. Now, here we were, Luther and I, joining voices with a larger group than ever we had at Northeast Camp, and singing some of those same songs that we used to sing with Mama playing the piano. We were singing with a pipe organ now, but the words were the same: words about a blessed assurance, and being led by Jesus, and about God's great faithfulness. We also sang a few new ones. One I learned that session and remains a favorite is the hymn Harry Emerson Fosdick wrote for the dedication of the new Riverside Church, "God of Grace and God of Glory." It could have been my state of mind – or state of soul – but I remember few words having such a profound impact on me as the words of that hymn: "Grant us wisdom, grant us courage, for the living of these days."

Dr. Robinson sent word to me that I was to meet the Board of Ministerial Training and Qualification during a lunch recess. Knowing my obsessive nature, I am reasonably sure that I was apprehensive about this review whose sole purpose was to see if I possessed the "gifts and graces to fulfill the duties of a minister" in the Methodist Church. None of my tension was the result of thinking I would be subjected to the type of questioning that I had received from the Nazarene board.

The atmosphere in that college classroom was far removed from the one that greeted me weeks before in that Nazarene Church conference room. A few of the faces I can still see. Charlie Wallace was laughing and telling stories, something he did until he died just a few years back. John Buckheister was fine-tuning the back slapping skills that made him such a favorite of all the churches he served. Tall Paul Jones was working the room. No, I didn't know their names then. But theirs are the faces I can still see as I think back on that day when this room full of strangers welcomed me.

They acted out their welcome by voting unanimously to accept me – even though the Nazarene Seminary was at that time not accredited – with the stipulation that I would take courses in Methodist History and Church Polity. John Bayley Jones, the chair of the board, said that this action was a recommendation that would have to be voted on by the conference session. He assured me that there would be no problem, and then said, if the conference did vote to accept me, I would be ordained a deacon at the closing session of annual conference on Sunday afternoon.

The conference did vote me in, and I made a quick call to Wave. "I'm being ordained a deacon. I have no idea what that is, but they talk like it is something special. You will want to come." Neither of us remembers who kept the children for her trip to Western Maryland. Both of us decided that it had to be one of the young mothers in the church that we had told the truth about what we were up to.

Harold Lanman, one of the officials on the Board, took me aside and said, "Tom, I doubt if you have a clerical robe. You will need one for the ordination ceremony. You can use mine."

I remember little of that service. We sang another new hymn the Methodists taught me,

> "O, young and fearless prophet, of ancient Galilee,
>
> Thy life is still a summons to serve humanity;
>
> To make our thoughts and actions less prone to please the crowd,
>
> To stand with humble courage for truth with hearts uncowed."

I remember feeling Bishop John Wesley Lord's hand pressing down on my head as I placed my hand on a Bible and he instructed me to "take thou authority to preach the Gospel." What I also remember feeling, as Wave and I drove back to Easton to finish packing for our move to Washington, D. C., is that I was now, officially, not only a duly credentialed minister in the Church of Jesus Christ, but also a minister in a branch of that church that was trying to live out the hope of its founder who believed that both head and heart had to be joined in any faith worth having.

By the time we moved into the parsonage of the North Carolina Avenue/Wilson Memorial Methodist Churches, more of my family had decided to join Luther and me in our exodus from the Nazarene Church. Mama, my sisters Jane and Ruth, and their husbands, Charles and

Billy, all joined St. John's Methodist Church in Seaford – just a block or two away from the church that my Dad had built. My sister Lucille and her husband Olen, joined Brookside Methodist Church in northern Delaware, and my sister Florine and her husband Irving also became Methodists. It is somewhat ironic that my sister Elizabeth was the lone holdout. "Sis", as Papa and Nannie Cowan called her, was their favorite. When the family moved to Delaware, and my grandparents' plans to keep her in Tennessee with them failed, part of Papa Cowan's good bye to her was the comment, "Now, Sis, don't you go off up there and let them make a 'holy roller' out of you." Elizabeth never became a 'holy roller'. She did, however, remain a faithful Nazarene until her death, and, I am convinced, never let go of her concern about the eternal destinies of not just her brothers and sisters, but her mother as well.

Wilson Memorial and North Carolina Avenue churches could not have been more welcoming. It had been a long time since they had such a young family living in the parsonage, and they doted on Tommy and Vicky. Both churches had been losing members to the "white flight" that was so much a part of the District of Columbia's life then. The decline had leveled off to a core of families, about half of which still lived on Capitol Hill, with the others driving in from Virginia. There were just a few children in the church school, and a very small youth group.

But the congregations were both larger than Orrick Methodist or Easton Nazarene. The sanctuaries had stained glass windows and pipe organs. There were acolytes to light the candles, and printed orders of worship. We prayed prayers of confession, affirmed our faith with historic creeds, and the North Carolina Avenue Church choir wasn't all that bad. I wore a choir robe until the pulpit gown the church bought for me was delivered. This was "church" as I had always wished it to be.

Luther and I enjoyed our time together. We attended seminary, and he would, on occasion stay with Wave and me instead of driving back to his churches in northern Maryland. Since I had to take the classes required for ordination, I decided to enroll in Wesley Seminary's Master of Sacred Theology program. The seminary functioned as a "halfway house" for Luther and me. It offered us safe passage into this newfound denominational world of ours. We made friends there, not just with the students, but with the professors as well. One of my professors, of all things, was a former Nazarene minister. He had been a president of one of the Nazarene colleges, and after receiving his Ph. D. from Boston University, joined the Methodist Church and eventually came to Wesley to teach systematic theology. The seminary librarian's father had been a prominent holiness evangelist. Luther and I spent many hours with Emily Chandler and Dr. Gilmore swapping Nazarene stories.

Life couldn't have been better. Not only was the salary higher than any I had ever received, the church also provided an automobile expense allowance. On top of what seemed to me a generous compensation package was added a furnished parsonage. And it was fun living on "the hill." A college friend came to visit and we went to the Senate chambers in the middle of one night to observe a filibuster in process. Trolleys ran just a block away on East Capitol Street, and Wave would take Vicky and Tommy with her on shopping trips downtown. At Christmas we would all ride down to see the beautifully decorated windows of Woodward and Lothrop and of Hecht's. Since the Chesapeake Bay Bridge had replaced the old Matapeake Ferry, home in Delaware and the resort beaches were just a few hours away.

I found that I liked being a preacher. No longer struggling with the "should I go, should I stay" questions, I could just go about the tasks of being a pastor to a couple of struggling inner city churches. Without having to walk gingerly around theological positions that I found untenable, my preaching began to focus on what I considered real life concerns. I had never dealt with the issue of race in a sermon, but how could I not do it now. Each Sunday I faced two congregations whose continued existences were in question because of the racially demographic changes that were occurring all around them. I was a twenty-seven year old kid who knew next to nothing about the "block-busting" tactics of realtors, nor of the fears that gripped older pensioners who loved their homes on the hill, planned to die there, and couldn't afford to move even if they had wanted to. So, I tried to read between their lines – lines that sometimes let the "N" word slip – and get at this dreaded fear of insecurity that gripped them; a fear, also of losing not just their neighborhood as they had known it, but their church community as well. I had to be true, though, to what I had been taught at home, by a mother who said "nigra" and a father who called black men "uncle". They had taught me, though, both "by precept and example", as the baptism ritual puts it, that the song I had learned in Sunday school, was true.

> "Jesus loves the little children, all the children of the world,
>
> Red and Yellow, Black and White, they are precious in his sight,
>
> Jesus loves the little children of the world"

If this was gospel truth, as I had been taught, then I had to find ways to obey the command my Bishop had given me at my ordination when he placed his hands on my head and told me to "take thou authority and preach the gospel."

"Speaking the truth in love" is not as easy as Jesus made it sound. God knows I tried, and I hope, with some measure of success. What really put it to the test was when the congregations and I got a notice of a meeting being held at Trinity Methodist Church which was within walking distance of the North Carolina Avenue Church. Two other Methodist Congregations were also invited.

It was at this meeting that the plan the bishop and his cabinet had for these five struggling Capitol Hill congregations was presented. Bits and pieces of it had become known; now the full story was told. The conference administration had determined that if these five churches – all within walking distance of each other – continued going their separate ways, eventually they would all die. The number of members moving to the suburbs would continue – probably increase. And it was just a matter of time before they would all have to close their doors. Not since 1939 had they been three separate denominations: Methodist Episcopal, Methodist Church South, and Methodist Protestant. The time had come to live out the 1939 Plan of Union.

What I did not know until then was that my coming to the two churches was the first step in the direction of implementing this plan. Multiple church "circuits" had been a part of Methodism from the beginning. There were numerous circuits in the Baltimore Conference. Mine was the first city circuit. The second step in the plan would be the creation of a Capitol Hill Parish. The five churches would function like a circuit, with the exception that instead of one pastor there would be two.

The congregations were told that Methodist Church law gave bishops the authority to arrange churches without the expressed approval of the churches involved. When Epworth Church, the largest of the five with a thousand members, and not convinced that they, like the rest of us, might someday soon cease to be, made it clear that bishops' prerogative notwithstanding, they were not going down without a fight. The conference administration relented, and the creation of a four church parish became the operative plan.

Wilson Memorial, the smallest of the churches, and located in the farthest reaches of the gentrification that was occurring on the hill, accepted their fate; actually seemed rather excited about the whole thing. The North Carolina Avenue congregation was something else again. Their roots were in the Methodist Protestant tradition – the split that occurred in the middle of the 19th century, not over slavery, but over the power of bishops. When they broke off from the mother church, they left all the bishops behind. So, North Carolina Avenue vowed not to have any part of this parish plan.

I had learned to love these people. L. D. Hiser, Mammy and Pappy Hipsley, Mr. Moseley, all parent and grandparent figures, wrapped their arms around us, and, L. D. Hiser, especially, tutored me in the ways of organizational Methodism. Reminiscent of my father, he ran the church. He sat on practically every committee, chairing two or three of them. The last few ministers preceding me were counting the days until their retirement, and, it seemed to me, had been quite willing to have someone run the show. It certainly was not a big show, so for them, apparently, letting L. D. run it was of little or no consequence.

Given my young age and lack of experience, L. D. was an enormous help to me. And the people trusted him. His surrogate leadership of the church posed no threat to me, until the Sunday in church school that he announced a meeting to be held at his house that evening for all those opposed to the conference's parish plans. Although I had no strong feelings either about the advisability of establishing the parish or about my need to play the good soldier and support my superiors, I felt the meeting was not a good idea, and I couldn't let it be held. And painful as it was, that's what I said to L. D. Had I not liked him so much, and had he not been such a big help to me here at the beginning of my life as a Methodist preacher, it would have been so much less painful to say. I had no authority to tell anyone they couldn't invite guests to their house for any reason whatsoever. L. D. might not have wanted to complicate my life or to not put me at cross- purposes with my superiors – whatever the reason, the meeting was not held.

As the year progressed, North Carolina Avenue Church, though decidedly unhappy about their "arranged" future, learned to live with it. Talking about the parish arrangement got put aside and we all went on about our regular duties. It achieved priority status in the spring with the official announcement that a Dr. Edward Bradley Lewis was being appointed to be the senior minister of the newly formed Capitol Hill Parish. The other part of the announcement, in much smaller print, was that the Reverend Thomas C. Starnes would be Dr. Lewis' assistant.

District Superintendent Robinson fleshed out the details: Dr. Lewis would, technically, be the pastor of all four churches. In reality, his primary responsibilities would be Trinity and Waugh, two of the larger churches. Mine would be the two I had had for the previous year. He would preach at Trinity and Waugh for the first three Sundays in the month, and I would preach at Wilson Memorial and North Carolina Avenue on those Sundays. Then on the fourth Sunday we would switch. I have no idea what happened in the months of five Sundays.

Through Fear to Faith

I met Ed Lewis at the Annual Conference session in June. He was excited about moving to Capitol Hill. Two years at the large suburban parish he was leaving had been long enough. His tastes were more urban, he told me. There probably was more to his decision to accept the bishop's offer than just his being more at home in the city. His predecessor minister there was well liked, an excellent preacher, and strikingly handsome. The church was also filled with young families. This, no doubt, caused Ed's unmarried status to take on a higher degree of importance for him than might otherwise have been the case. He was quite personable, full of energy, and determined to staunch the bleeding in these four near death congregations.

I enjoyed working with him. It nettled my two congregations – more so North Carolina Avenue than Wilson Memorial – that the "assistant pastor" title given to me in the parish plan became "assistant to the pastor" when the Senior Minister moved in. North Carolina Avenue members – some of them anyway – made it known that I would be their one and only pastor. Other than that, the transition went very well.

Ed began to market his enthusiasm. He was forever saying to me "nothing breeds success like success." And we started having some successes. He advertised us as being "In the shadow of the nation's capitol." It would have taken a rather long shadow even to reach Waugh Church, the closest of the four to the capitol building. But it was good public relations. The Trinity Church parsonage was remodeled as office space. Ed took the large front bedroom as his office. Bookcases were built in. I was given a back bedroom, plenty large enough, also with built in bookshelves. Sitting in a swivel chair with feet up on a desk larger than any I had ever had, surrounded by bookshelves waiting for me to fill them, and a secretary downstairs ready to do my bidding, all seemed to be right with my little preaching world.

However, it was while sitting in that swivel chair with my feet on the desk one night in early October, reading Leslie Weatherhead's book, <u>The Christian Agnostic</u>, that the foundations of this little preaching world of mine were shaken.

Chapter 9

"If you bring forth what is within you, what you bring forth will save you. If you do not bring forth what is within you, what you do not bring forth will destroy you."

Gospel of Thomas

There was no apparent reason for the fear that engulfed me that October evening as I sat at the desk reading. I was adjusting to my life as a Methodist minister. Ed and I were getting along rather nicely, and classes at Wesley were going well. In addition, Wave had just returned from the hospital with our third child – this one planned – Floyd Duncan, named after his two grandfathers. I was reading about belief in God – not at all an unfamiliar subject for me – when a sense of terror gripped me. Never had I had this exact feeling.

The closest anything came to it was the fear and dread I felt when the evangelist convinced me that, at age twelve, I had committed the unpardonable sin and, as he put it, "sinned away my day of grace." It is true that fear was not a stranger to me in my growing up years. Diseases of various sorts were my phobias of choice. Lockjaw, rabies, brain tumor, heart disease, all at one time or another fed my anxious mind. The unpardonable sin made another brief appearance during the opening convocation at college. Here again, it was an evangelist who came to the school for what was billed as a Fall convocation, but was really nothing more than a revival meeting, who, once more, convinced me that at the age of eighteen, I had indeed "sinned away my day of grace." When that fear ran its course, others took its place: fear of closed places, fear of open places and, in varying degrees of intensity, fear that I could, at any moment, drop dead of a heart attack.

However, my fears never got in the way of my leading a very active life. I never gave into them. They were my secret. All the while I was visiting every doctor on both sides of Elm Avenue, the street that led into Eastern Nazarene College's campus, seeking reassurance that my heart was sound, I was playing football and basketball, working thirty hours a week, singing every weekend with a quartet, establishing myself as a rather serious student, and thought of as a fun loving, happy go lucky guy, with not a care in the world.

But these were all fears of "something." The fear and dread that settled in on me that October night in 1960, though, was of absolutely nothing. Chest pains would have come as a welcome relief. All I knew was that I was terrified for no apparent reason.

Mama was staying with us to help Wave take care of baby Floyd, as well as Vicky and Tommy. I said nothing to anyone when I got to the house that night. Fears were always mine and mine alone. I snuggled up to Wave in bed, as I had snuggled up close to my Dad on that church pew the night my anxious little ears heard the evangelist telling me that God had kissed me off, but closeness to Wave, like closeness to my father, gave me no assurance of safety. It was my first sleepless night ever.

The sunshine of the next morning brought no relief. Doing as I had always done, I decided to tough it out. The occasion called for heroics on my part. Wave was the one who needed attention – that's why Mama was there. And where was the cigar passing excitement that the birth of this darling little boy demanded? I needed to finish Erich Fromm's book, <u>The Art of Loving</u>, in preparation for the presentation I was to make at the afternoon seminar I was taking at Wesley. And with no backlog of sermons built up, I needed to piece something together to preach on Sunday.

Whether I worked on any of this that day, I don't recall. What I do know is that for the second night running I didn't close my eyes. And the next morning it was clear to me that I was in a place unlike any I had ever experienced. I needed help, desperately, and for me the logical place to turn, as it had been all through college, and as it had always been for Mama to help her handle her anxieties, was a doctor. A general practitioner had been recommended to us, and I made an appointment.

The difference this time was that I did not slip off to the doctor as I had during college, choosing to suffer in silence. I have no memory of the words I chose to convey to Wave or Mama how fearful I was. However I phrased my concern, Wave got the message. Maybe we had been married long enough for her to read between my lines. Years later, when I told her that all I was convinced of at the time is that I had finally gone over the edge, and that I would be committed to St. Elizabeth's Hospital just a few blocks away, she allowed as how they had been her thoughts as well.

The doctor was a kind, consoling, fatherly type – the kind I always hoped to find whenever I went out on my physician searches. Two things I remember about that appointment: the medicine he prescribed, and what he said to me after he told me that I was in excellent physical condition. The medicine was a bad choice. It was an anti-depressant

— Elavil, I think — designed to elevate my mood. Hyper as I was, the last thing my mood needed was to be taken to an even higher level. His words to me, though, were priceless. He told me a story about a young patient of his who had given in to his fears, and for years thereafter, never left his house.

I marshaled as much will power as I possessed, and, popping the prescribed pill, went about my business. But the dread hung on. So after a few more nights of fitful sleep, and days filled with thoughts of coming days certain to be spent in the safe confines of St. Elizabeth's, I took my first step ever toward a doctor who might closely examine something other than my body.

In college, I had made a feint in the direction of psychological help. A young professor had come to the psychology department, and I remember nothing of any presenting symptoms I offered as a reason for him to meet with me. He suggested lunch, and the only memory I have of that experience is that he ate a piece of apple pie. If I bared my soul to him there in the midst of banging trays and the noisy chattering of students, I don't remember it. We never met again, and the only reason I mention this incident here is to indicate that even back in those college days, at some level, I must have known that it just could be that the healing I was seeking couldn't be found in those often frequented doctors' offices that lined both sides of Elm Avenue.

Now, just as in college, only in a much more desperate state of mind, I reached out to a professor. Dr. Eugene Ferguson taught pastoral counseling at the Seminary, and was the professor for the seminar I was taking. I called him, and told him little more than that I was terrified and needed help. He gave me the number of a clinical psychologist that Wesley Seminary retained to test incoming students and offer therapy at a reduced rate to those students who wanted it. I remember asking him if he thought I was going crazy. Knowing the difference between psychosis and neurosis – a difference I did not as yet know – he tried to assure me that I was not going crazy. And then he said words that I would doggedly cling to in the months ahead: "You will get better. In days to come these clouds will lift."

Since this is a "faith" memoir, not a life story, written with the friends in mind from those long ago Nazarene years, who not only have not kept the Nazarene faith, but have not kept any religious faith at all, and who want to know not only how I managed to remain a person of faith – a preacher even – and what, on earth have I preached. So, to keep true to that aim, I now want to move from a more or less chronological telling of my story, to a more thematic approach.

And therapy is the theme of this part. One can never know such things for sure, "God moves in mysterious ways," and all that, but I have serious doubts whether I would have remained a preacher, or, for that matter, kept the faith, were it not for the therapists who have been my guides.

And the first of these saviors of mine is the one Dr. Ferguson told me to call, Dr. Michael Finn. Around seminary, behind his back, of course, he was known as "Mickey Finn." He had a hint of a stutter, and on some of those Wednesdays and Fridays I could hear the sound of his fingernail clipper behind me, as I lay stretched out on his couch. There were even stories of his drifting off to sleep in the middle of a session. He could have taken a nap or two during those four years that I rambled on. All I know is that slowly but surely, week in week out, whatever he and I did together in that room in downtown Baltimore caused the fear in my life to shrink to a manageable level, and the storm clouds part just enough to let some sunshine through.

He began by getting me to a place where I could see what might be behind that paralyzing fear. So, I was reading about God? Who's been God for you all these years? Daddy? The Nazarene Church? Daddy's dead now, and, for you, so is the Nazarene Church. Both of my giant security blankets were gone, he suggested. Is it any wonder then that I was afraid? He was the first to tell me about stress factors, not all of which are bad: births of children, moving, taking a new job. Even enjoyable experiences, like moving to a new and exciting job, welcoming a new son into your life, are stressful. He suggested a label for my life long fears. They were, according to him, my "talisman." I admit I never understood this completely. His judgment was that I needed to be afraid of something to protect me from an even graver danger. He also said that fear had been so much a part of my life – a sort of secret pal – that I was more comfortable having it around. It took me a while to admit the element of truth in this therapeutic guess of his.

Fear wasn't all that we talked about in those sessions. A few months of my not paying him on time, led into some hours being spent looking at why I did not pay other bills when due, or put money in parking meters. Since neither paying bills on time nor plugging parking meters seemed to have anything to do with the availability of funds, Dr. Finn suggested that it might be some delayed adolescent rebellion against authority on my part. A therapeutic stretch, I thought then and still do, but I've put money in meters ever since, and any late payment of bills has been due to lack of funds. One day when I was remorsefully listing all the items on my "to do list" that I had as yet not crossed off, he said, "Why don't you shove a broom up your ass and sweep the chancel while you are preaching." With him I was able to admit, for the first time, how devastating it was for me to receive just one word of criticism. It was also in his office that it became apparent to me how large a role pleasing others played in the way I chose to live my life.

About one month into therapy, when my emotions were still raw, and the last thing I needed was another stress factor to enter my life, Dr. Robinson, my district superintendent, told me that I was being transferred. He said that the Bishop and his cabinet felt that I would be a good fit for a circuit of three churches in northern Maryland. The minister there had left, rather suddenly, leaving his wife and two small sons behind, and it wouldn't be good to leave those churches without a pastor for any length of time. Besides, the Capitol Hill Parish had voted to become a single church, Capitol Hill Methodist, and worship together using the Trinity church until a new church could be built on the Trinity Church site. Since I was not needed to preach in my two churches, I was expendable.

My first Sunday at the North Harford Charge, was January 1, 1961. It was a hectic move, coming as it did close on the heels of Christmas, and given the fact that Floyd was just three months old, and I was still not all that sure that St. Elizabeth's would not be my place of residence in the not too distant future. However, there were some advantages to the move. Luther and Joyce were in the neighboring community, so Luther and I could ride to seminary together, and Wave and Joyce would be company for each other. Another plus was the parsonage – a large country house surrounded by a lawn and shaded by a few good size maple trees. Although Lincoln Park was just a couple blocks from the Washington parsonage, having a park in your own yard would be much better.

It wasn't long, though, until issues of whether or not being a preacher was the way I wanted to spend my life began to dominate my fifty-minute hours. Specifically, I wondered if mine had been an authentic call from God, or whether or not it was connected with my wanting to please others, especially Daddy, who, some of us in his family felt, was, at heart, a frustrated preacher. There were more than just a few weeks when I would, while lying on Finn's couch, leave the ministry, and feel absolutely euphoric with the thought. I would then go home and write Sunday's sermon and come back to therapy the following week and jump ship all over again. Part of this, no doubt, had to do with the emotional strain I was still under. Part of it had to do with the workload. I preached three times every Sunday morning at services on the hour which necessitated rushing from one to the other, with no break in between, and all three of the churches multiple boards and committees were functioning, which meant that I had three of everything to attend.

While all this is true, and, no doubt played a role in my disquiet with my calling to be a minister, there was another factor present. Dublin Church, the largest of the three, had a rather strong contingent of conservative Methodists who were wielding a lot of influence. There had been a minister there, years before who was, for all practical purposes, a Nazarene at heart. He was independently wealthy, and used his funds to send a few of the youth in the church off to college at Asbury in Wilmore, Kentucky – one of Methodism's most conservative schools. These graduates were now in positions of leadership and they still worshipped "Brother Luce". Brother Luce had even had evangelists come and hold revivals. The interior of Dublin Church, with its composition board walls, looked like so many of the Nazarene Churches that I had sung in during my college summers. They supported neither the Methodist College in our area nor the Methodist Camp, citing Brother Luce's evaluation that neither place was Christian. Actually, as I now recall, they used the word godless to describe them both. Dublin Church did not even use the Methodist Church's Sunday school curriculum. Some criticism was personal: I wore a robe, I had the altar candles lighted using acolytes instead of ushers with cigarette lighters, and I did not preach the Bible. This was not the promised land of Methodism as I had thought it would be.

What kept me steady, along with my afternoons in Dr. Finn's office, was Emory Church, the one where I concluded my Sunday morning rounds. They did not share Dublin's anti-Methodist views, they thought I was God's gift to them, and their picturesque high-steeple church, bright and airy, came as a welcome relief each Sunday morning. And the longer I stayed, the more apparent it became that the majority of the Dublin members were not worshippers at the altar of Brother Luce.

Something else began to stir in me that made me question my fitness for the ministry. I developed a phobic reaction to being in the pulpit. Preaching became sheer agony. I would cling to the pulpit for fear that my knees would buckle. There was only one explanation for this, I would tell Dr. Finn: I don't want to be there. This is my body reacting to this imprisonment in a life that I don't want.

Round and round I would go in my sessions. I even flew to Wisconsin to interview for a job with Wave's brother who was an executive with a major industrial firm. He offered me a job, but I flew home and immediately began working on next Sunday's sermon.

Over time, the clouds lifted, and I settled into my life as a Methodist preacher. I don't remember my first session with Dr. Finn in the fall of 1960. I do remember well our last session in the spring of 1964. It was a sunny day, and when I entered the office and was getting ready to stretch out on the couch, he told me to sit in the chair facing him. We chatted amiably about the road we had traveled together. He had never given me any diagnosis, so I asked him what had been wrong with me back when he and I first met. He said that I had experienced a full-blown, no holds barred, anxiety attack. I left that downtown Baltimore office walking on air.

The next time I heard from him was eight years later in a note congratulating me on being elected chair of the Conference Board of Ministry, a rather prestigious board that determined who would be accepted into the Methodist ministry. He sent me another letter of congratulations when I was appointed to the largest church in the conference, and then another when I was asked to serve on the Bishop's cabinet. His death in an automobile accident a few years later put an end to that good intention of mine to make sure he knew how indebted I was to him.

When I left Dr. Finn's office that bright spring day in 1964, I was not cured. I was healed, though. For during those four years of couch work, I was guided into an understanding that anxiety, for me, for whatever reason, was an incurable disease. Maybe it was my talisman to ward off deeper and more basic fears – say of abandonment – or maybe even just the way I am genetically wired. What I also came to understand was that I need not fear the fear, and when faced, fears tend to shrink in size.

This was insight enough to carry me through some rather hectic days that followed. Lightning struck the steeple of Emory Church early one Sunday morning, and within a few hours all that remained of that lovely community landmark was some charred rubble. At the time this "act of God" – as insurance adjustors call such things – occurred, Dublin Church was building an educational building. Progress on that project had been hampered by a lawsuit brought by a wealthy local resident who said we were building the addition over five of her long dead relatives who were resting in not so honored glory in unmarked graves. Emory Church constructed a new building and Dublin Church, after winning its court case, completed its' addition.

All this was accomplished with no panic attacks or the return of any serious bouts of anxiety. And that's the way it went for the next ten years. During that time I was moved to a parish in suburban Washington, D.C. The church was in a newly created Leavitt Town in Prince George's County Maryland. It was a dream appointment. Leavitt was building ninety new homes a week, and Methodism was getting its proportioned share of the church going market. Two hundred new members joined during my first year. The average age of the community was thirty-four, which resulted in the membership of St. Matthew's Church consisting of young families, fresh out of college, buying their first homes (the smallest Leavitt house could be bought for $11,000) and starting families. Besides all this, for the first time ever, I had a full time secretary.

I navigated my way through school busing for the purposes of racial integration and the Vietnam War, losing a few military families and some "lace curtain" liberals, who were okay with integration in principle but not in particular, if that meant that their children might have to be bused to a predominately black school. We went through a struggle to get a new sanctuary built, coming as it did at just the time in the early seventies when interest rates climbed to an unheard of ten percent.

My Sunday morning pulpit shakes stayed with me, but no longer did I see them as proof that I really didn't want to be doing what my ordaining Bishop had given me authority to do: "preach the Word." For me, it was stage fright -- just plain old performance anxiety. Besides, I had come to enjoy preaching, both the delivery and the preparation involved.

Therapy never entered my mind. For me, that was a closed chapter in my life. I was anxious at times, but who wouldn't be. St. Matthew's was increasing in size. It had doubled in membership during the first four years I was there. I had no ministerial staff assistance. I did, however, have capable lay volunteers who assisted in the education department.

But the parish ministry – the caring and nurturing of the congregation – was solely my responsibility. I took no weekday off, telling Wave that Saturday was my day off. But few Saturdays were really free. My days were long usually ending at nine after an evening meeting.

Every now and again I would reach into my talisman bag and pull out my old standby – heart trouble. Palpitations, which I had experienced even as I played basketball, became my obsession. So back to the doctor I would go only to have the EKG's and stress tests ordered tell me what I had been hearing for all my growing up years that my heart was in good shape.

It was not fear that pushed me in the direction of further headwork: it was my beginning to question whether Wave and I were a good fit. Ours had never been an easy-going carefree relationship. But once through the courtship – a courtship that I ended once – it looked like we would make it. Being the strong-willed, bright, over achieving persons that both of us are, conflict was to be expected. However, seventeen years into our marriage, I found myself wondering if, in fact, we were really suited for the "'til death do we part" clause of the marriage contract.

The details of all this will stay with Wave and me. All I will say is that it became obvious that we needed help. So we turned to the closest resource available, the counseling center our local clergy association had established in cooperation with the Pastoral Counseling and Consultation Centers of Greater Washington. Dr. Mark Friehage, the therapist assigned to the Bowie center, was in the process of exiting the Roman Catholic priesthood. Wave and I saw Mark together and separately for about two years. Because of my professional relationship with him, it was difficult for me to enter into anything approaching a therapeutic relationship. Wave, on the other hand, found these two years helpful. Whatever happened between Mark and us those two years, the truth remains that for the first time Wave and I took a long hard look at our life together and decided that what brought us together in the first place was worth holding on to.

Six months after completion of St. Matthew's new sanctuary, the Bishop appointed me to one of the largest churches in the Baltimore/Washington Conference. The membership at St. Matthew's had almost tripled in my seven year tenure there. All this had occurred during some of the most tumultuous times in our society. I had managed to keep the lid on a church filled with more than its share of retired colonels and FBI agents even though I was an outspoken critic of the Vietnam War and a worshipper at the feet of Martin Luther King, Jr.

I was thrilled when the call came asking me if I would be willing to go to First Church Hyattsville. Wave was taking a class, working on her Master's Degree at the University of Maryland, and I was preparing dinner. Just after I put the receiver down, I took a jar of mustard from the refrigerator. It wasn't just any jar. It was the giant economy size. The top had not been secured, and just as I got the jar out of the refrigerator, that huge golden bomb went crashing to the floor. Not only did it make its mark on the indoor/outdoor carpeting that was all the rage in those middle 70's years, it shot mustard and shards of glass into the more expensively carpeted dining room. I said the only "bad" word I ever heard my mother utter, "shit", and the kids helped me clean up the mess, and listened as I excitedly told them that their Dad had just been asked to go to a very large church. Vicky was delighted with the news. She would be leaving Bowie, and home, anyway, to go to college. It was Tommy who brought reality into the picture by reminding me that he had one more year in high school and would like nothing better than to finish with the kids he had been in school with since the fourth grade.

When Wave returned that evening, she shared in my excitement, and after we got special permission from the Superintendent of Schools for Tommy to remain at Bowie High School for his senior year, he shared in my excitement as well.

One of our painful memories is that neither of us thought that Floyd might also like to stay in Bowie and finish out his last year of junior high with the same group of kids he had been in school with since the second grade.

It was a dream come true for me. In those early days when Luther and I would ride back and forth to seminary from our parishes in northern Maryland, there was an exit off the Baltimore/Washington Parkway for Hyattsville, a small close-in-to D. C. town that had experienced rapid growth in the first wave of postwar suburban sprawl. After a while we learned about First Church Hyattsville – 2500 members; the first million dollar church building in the conference – and each time we passed the cut-off sign for Hyattsville on the parkway, I dreamed what seemed an impossible dream at the time: that one day, I might be the pastor of that very large and prestigious church.

Seared into my brain had always been this desire to be number one – to go to the head of the class – to be somebody. Perhaps it can be traced to those Nazarene growing up years when I never felt as if I belonged. Whatever its genesis, I had it. Not only had I dreamed of being the pastor of the largest church, I wanted to be known as the best preacher. Now I had achieved at least one of those goals, and my reputation as a fairly decent preacher was spreading. Sometimes I allowed myself to dream about getting elected a bishop. Talk about being number one. In Methodism nothing trumps having the title of bishop stuck on to your name. And when Wave told me that my district superintendent's wife had told her that this move could put me on the fast track leading to the episcopacy, I thought, "Who knows, it just could be."

I felt no hesitancy at moving into this responsibility. Just seven years removed from a country circuit, never having had any staff to supervise, and considered a bit young to be going to the head of the preaching class, I moved in without skipping a beat. Staff I had a plenty. There were two ministers besides me. I had a full time associate, and a part time retired minister to handle most of the visitation, especially among the sick and homebound. I had a full time education director, a full time music director, a pre-school director, a kitchen coordinator, building superintendent, three custodians, an office manager and two secretaries.

I loved it all. The worship there was a glorious experience. The organist was considered one of the best in the Washington area, as was the giant pipe organ. The choir was a sixty-voice ensemble that sang the finest music. The pulpit was, in the words of Isaiah "high and lifted up", fitting Melville's prow of a ship description, and it faced head on into one of the most beautiful faceted glass windows I have ever seen. And sitting out in front of me on most Sunday mornings were seven or eight hundred people. I was in high clover.

All went well. The church was not as rapidly growing as had been the case with St. Matthews. People were not moving into Hyattsville at the same rate that they had been moving into Bowie. Hyattsville families, especially the young ones, were moving on up to places further out, like Bowie. And given the age of the church, few weeks passed without a funeral or two. Truth was we had to take in one hundred new members a year just to stay even. But it was an exciting church. It had a social conscience. It had established the first youth runaway house in the area. All kinds of human services were listed in its outreach budget. Space was provided in the building for a counseling center.

Mama came to worship one Sunday. She was now living in an assisted living facility, her doctor having determined that her congestive heart failure had reached the point where she could no longer live alone. The Sunday she came the associate and I had agreed to preach a dialog sermon. He preached one Sunday a month and this was his day. Just before he entered the pulpit, as we were singing the hymn before the sermon, I left the chancel, and made my way around through the lower level and came into the narthex. Jack had only said an introductory sentence or two, when I entered the rear of the sanctuary and walked down the center aisle shouting "just a minute, just a minute." I went to the lectern and Jack and I continued our dialog on the meaning of worship. After the service Mama couldn't wait to tell me that just as I had come bursting into the sanctuary, the woman sitting in front of her leaned over to the woman sitting next to her and said, "Has he lost his senses?"

I wish I had preached that day. Mama never was much for tinkering with orders of worship. Her preacher back in Seaford had brought a phonograph into the pulpit one Sunday and proceeded to play "Winchester Cathedral." Mama was beside herself when she said to me, "Thomas, don't you ever do anything silly like that." She didn't seem too upset with what Jack and I had done to the sermon time. I do wish I had preached though, because it was the last time Mama ever worshipped with me. She died on November 5, 1975.

The family all gathered for the funeral in St. John's Methodist Church in Seaford, and for the burial in Bethel Church cemetery beside Daddy and Benton. Mama's death was not unexpected. She had been in and out of the hospital for months, so it came as no great shock. I returned from the funeral and went on with my busy life. One afternoon I was walking through a downstairs hall at the church, and Frances Dooley, a woman about Mama's age, whose son was also a Methodist preacher, came up beside me and putting her arm around me said, "Tom, I guess you know that you've just lost your best friend." And with her words still hanging there, in mid-air, the first wave of panic since those early Dr. Finn days swept over me.

The next sequence of events is lost to me. I do know that once again I felt the need to talk this through. We had not as yet settled on a family physician in Hyattsville; I was still seeing our Bowie doctor. He referred me to a psychiatrist whose specialty was family systems therapy. Our sessions consisted of my giving him family information – brothers, sisters, parents, grandparents – and his making a family tree out of all this data on a sheet of newsprint. I don't remember much of my time with him. Some of it must have been spent with Mama's death, and also with my sister Elizabeth's illness. Just months before Mama's death, Elizabeth was diagnosed with cervical cancer. In her early fifties, she had not been as diligent as her sisters felt she should have been with regular check-ups. In those days, at least in that section of the country, Doctors did not often trust patients with the truth. After her surgery, Elizabeth's doctors did, however, give the impression at least, using such phrases as "we did the best we could", that her fight with cancer would be a losing battle.

Which it was; she died the following May. It was a sunny spring day that all of us Starnes' children, with our families, gathered in the Salisbury, Maryland Nazarene Church for Elizabeth's going home service. It was the first time any of us had been inside a Nazarene Church since we made our grand exodus almost twenty years previous. Someone else was in Elizabeth's spot on the piano bench and this someone else played a song not unfamiliar to that piano, a song Elizabeth had played countless times, accompanying her husband John, as he sang,

> "There waits for me a glad tomorrow,
>
> Where gates of pearl swing open wide,
>
> And when I pass this vale of sorrow,
>
> I'll rest upon the other side.
>
> Someday, beyond the reach of mortal kin,
>
> Someday, God only knows just where and when,
>
> The wheels of mortal life shall all stand still,
>
> And I shall go to dwell on Zion's Hill."

I agree with almost nothing the Reverend Jerry Falwell says or stands for, but I will always be grateful for what he did when my sister died. After the loss of their first child at birth, Elizabeth and John were blessed with a son. Jacky was not college material, but had the voice of an angel. Falwell's Liberty College in Lynchburg, Virginia, accepted him and he made a name for himself singing in the college choir. Elizabeth and John were not major donors to the college. However, this did not stop Falwell from loading the choir up on his private plane and sending them off to sing at Jacky's mother's funeral.

In just a matter of months, death had not only taken away the last person who stood between us children and the great beyond, our mother, but had also reached its clammy hand down and taken one of us. It's true that Benton had died almost twenty-five years before, but he had already lived longer than expected. Florine's husband, Irving, had also died in the February preceding Mama's death in November, but he wasn't one of us Starnes kids; and besides, he had struggled with diabetes for years.

All this must have been what the psychiatrist and I talked about as he hung his stick figures up on my family tree. Soon after Elizabeth's death, and feeling that family system's therapy might not be the way to reach my soul's disquiet, I terminated with him. How soon this occurred before death dropped the other shoe on Elizabeth's family, I don't know. But when that shoe dropped, or, to get more specific, when they found her husband John dead in the bed one morning in December, just six months after Elizabeth's death, at age 54, I knew it was time for me to try and find another Michael Finn. And yes, the Falwell plane, loaded with the college choir made one more trip to the little Nazarene church in Salisbury, Maryland.

Do you recall Dr. Paul Johnson's "slender threads" that I referred to in a previous chapter? This was the phrase he coined to describe those times in his life when he met just the right person who steered him in just the right direction. My slender thread came in the person of a pastoral counselor who was supervising my work in a course I was taking on pastoral psychotherapy. In one of my sessions with him, I asked if he knew a good therapist. He gave me two names. He liked them both he said, and thought the woman would be good for me. On second thought, though, perhaps Bob Kirsch would be a better fit. I took his advice and made an appointment.

Unlike it was with Dr. Finn, I remember my first session with Dr. Kirsch. His office was on the fourth floor of the Topaz Apartments in downtown Bethesda, Maryland. After a brief discussion about the terms of the only therapeutic contract he would agree to, Bob asked me why I was there. I do not remember any of the words I used, but after just a few sentences, he interrupted with a question. How do you feel right now, he asked? I said I didn't know; that hanging a label on my feelings had always been a toughie for me. Growing up in my family, I explained, where feelings were graded, and some, even, you weren't supposed to admit having, you learned to not pay all that much attention to them. He kept asking what I was feeling at this moment, until finally, almost in a whisper, I said, "I'm scared." He acted as if he hadn't heard me. "What," he asked. "Say it louder." "I'm scared", I said in a little louder voice. He persisted with a string of louder and louder "what's" until I was screaming at the top of my lungs "I'm scared." After what was for me my first ever, primal scream, I started to cry, and Bob thanked me for the gift of an honest emotion. The best way I have found to describe this experience is to say it was like a cap had been unscrewed from the top of my head and all that anxiety and dread that had been nesting in there for years had come flying out.

When our time was up that first day, Bob gave me an assignment. He told me to read Tolstoy's short story, "The Death of Ivan Ilych" and to buy a copy of Alan Watts little book, <u>The Wisdom of Insecurity</u>. It had not taken him long to see that what was scaring me to death was in fact death; that my anxiety was not just the result of four deaths in the family in the matter of months. It was the specter of my own mortality that had me on edge.

Bob was on retainer with me, off and on, until he died twenty years later. Both of us seekers, he only two years older, I like to think we learned from each other. Born into the Jewish faith, Christianity fascinated him. His first move out of the faith of his father was to attend All Souls Unitarian Church in Washington just to listen to its outstanding minister, E. Powell Davies. When I first met him, he had moved on to the Episcopal Church, feeling he was ready for more of the historic Christian faith and liturgy. Just a few years before he died, he found his final faith home in the Orthodox Church. Even the Episcopalians could not satisfy his faith and liturgical hungers.

After four months of twice a week sessions, Bob thought that group therapy would be good for me. This was not something that interested me in the least. I was making significant progress – or so it seemed to me – in these one-on-one hours. Why change it? Each day I was learning to accept the central truth of Alan Watts' The Wisdom of Insecurity: that insecurity is a part of life, and all of our attempts to become more secure only serve to make us less secure. This little book breathed new life into the words of Jesus that I had grown up with: "Whoever would save his life must lose it." Watts called this the "law of reverse effort," by which he meant, "If you lie on your back and try to float, you sink; but if you just lie on your back, you float." Over time I was learning to do this with the anxiety; just let it be. Eventually it will pass. At least it always has. One day my pulpit anxiety came up, and it occurred to me, I think for the first time, that it only affected me on Sunday morning. When I would speak in the evening, it was non-existent. Bob then asked me what my Sunday morning breakfasts were like. When I told him that they consisted of a donut or a sweet roll and two or three cups of coffee, followed by a cigarette or two, he suggested that I change my pre-preaching meal. He recommended an egg and a glass of milk. With that simple change of Sunday morning breakfast fare, my pulpit shakes were gone, leaving me with no physical reason for feeling that the ministry was not for me.

We covered other territory in those times together. I still wasn't convinced that Wave was the one for me. Maybe I had married my father, I would tell him. In college, perhaps, I wasn't mature enough to make it on my own, and I needed that firm controlling parent hand or God knows what I might have made of my life. I knew enough of transactional analysis to say that Wave and I never had adult to adult transactions; ours were usually parent to child, with Wave being the parent. Bob would listen, and always follow with a version of this comment, "all that could be, Wave might not be the one for you, but if you must part, you should not part as strangers," meaning, of course, that she and I needed to spend considerably more time getting to know each other.

My group sessions are a blur. I remember bits and pieces, even specific comments made on some days. Spending ninety minutes a week together, for three years, with essentially the same core group, one would think I would remember more. I don't. What I do know is that for the first time in my life I was forced to open up – to bare my soul – in the presence of others. These others would not allow me to stay disengaged, or, to give my usual glib answer, generally a quip. Over time we learned to sense when one of us was hurting, and, most of the time, kindly, but not always kindly, insist on being allowed to help them carry their load. It was here I had to learn to accept truth – even harsh truth – spoken in love and concern for me. I do not remember my final day with the group, nor do I remember my final day with Bob.

And it is really of no consequence because I was not through with Bob. Three years later, having just turned fifty, I came crawling back, for the craziest of reasons. My presenting symptom was weird obsessive thoughts: what if I started shouting obscenities during a sermon, or, what if I decided to drive my car into a tree. Bob assured me that such thoughts were not at all uncommon – even among the sanest of folks. He probably did an un-therapeutic type thing by telling me about the night he was holding his baby in an upstairs hall – gently rocking him in his arms – and suddenly thinking, wouldn't it be dreadful if I lost control and threw this child down the steps.

It took a few sessions before he turned my attention away from my obsessions – my talisman of choice – and pointed me in the direction of what he perceived to be at the center of my anxiety – growing older. Decade birthdays had never seemed difficult for me. My thirtieth came at the time we were being told not to trust anybody over thirty. That didn't seem to concern me. The same was true for what was perceived to be, at that time, the big one – number forty. So my fiftieth came and went without incident. But in those sessions, Bob opened my eyes a bit. The children had all finished college. Wave had her doctor's degree. Tommy had graduated from law school, and Vicky was seriously considering entering seminary. I had left First Church Hyattsville – much to the dismay of the church who felt that after six years together we had something good going – to become a district superintendent. I said yes to Bishop Mathews when he asked me to be a part of his cabinet, because I had determined early on that I would play this Methodist preaching game by the rules. And rule number one is that we go where we are sent.

The job was not a good fit for me. I missed preaching. I missed being a part of a faith community. More even than this, though, the old question that had consumed so many of my early hours with Dr. Finn, presented itself. Not in the same form, however. Now, it wasn't a question of whether preaching was God's will for my life or whether I was attempting to make one of my Dad's dreams come true. It was now a question of whether this is the way I wanted to spend the rest of my life, and if not, I'd better get cracking. Already the grains of sand in the bottom of my hourglass outnumbered the grains in the top.

Getting a Ph. D. had always been a bit of unfinished business for me. So I took a five-month study leave from my district superintendent position and enrolled in a doctoral program at Drew University. I lived at a Roman Catholic Retreat Center in nearby Morristown, New Jersey, named, of all things, St. Elizabeth's – proving perhaps that God does have a sense of humor. For the first time in my life I was able to study full time. The nuns in the center catered to my every wish, even making sure that the coffee pot stayed plugged in, and some cookies left over from their Bible study, so I could have some refreshments as I watched Monday night football on what was, for those days, a giant television. This was such a refreshing time for me. Never before in my undergraduate or graduate years had I spent whole days in a library. I passed the French qualifying exam – not all of us did – and having only one or two B's sharing transcript space with my A's, was convinced that I could do it.

And maybe that's all I needed; to know that if I wanted to get a Ph. D. I could do the work. I commuted the next semester, taking two seminars, while continuing my term on the bishop's cabinet. That was the last graduate course I took. The cost had something to do with it – both money and time. What also occurred was that as my anxiety lessened, life regained its interest; even the "same old same old" didn't look all that bad. I do not know that my hours with Bob brought about this change in me. Absent any other reason for it, he gets the credit.

Bob told me one day that when it came to personal issues, I was a slow learner. So he wasn't surprised to see me when I showed up at his door just a few months after my sixtieth birthday. Once again, it never occurred to me that my return to Bob had anything to do with my having lived to pass another of those decade birthdays – and a special one at that. It was early in his sixtieth year that my Dad died.

None of this was on my mind when I sank into that fourth floor office chair that had been mine off and on for fifteen years, and began to pour out my heart. Bob could have refused to see me, even been justified in tossing me out with a well deserved "enough is enough." He didn't. He listened as he and I meandered down those memory lanes that both of us knew so well. And little by little, he pointed me in the direction of my coming to the end of my professional trail. It wasn't my death that was unnerving me this time, he suggested; could it possibly be the death of some of the dreams I had had for myself that was the source of my unease.

Being elected Bishop was always there; more dream than reality, though. Perhaps not even a dream. A passing thought now and then might be a better way to characterize it. Truth was, the Baltimore/Washington Conference had not chosen a white man for the office since 1960, and he was not really one of us. Fred Holloway had been a member of our conference in years past, but had for some time been president of Drew University. The last three bishops elected from our conference had been two black men and one white woman. In 1984, as a delegate to the Jurisdictional Conference – the body that elects bishops – I was privileged to take our conference candidate, a friend and colleague, Forrest Stith, around to all the conference delegations, say a few words about why I thought he would make an excellent Bishop, and allow the delegates to ask a few questions. Forrest was the first African/American minister received into the Baltimore/Washington Conference. Bishop Mathews, the bishop who sent me to First Church Hyattsville at such an early age, and who selected me to be a part of his cabinet, took me aside as I was making the rounds of the conferences with Forrest in tow, and told me that if the church had been true to its faith one hundred years ago, someone would be offering me to the delegations as a candidate for the episcopacy. He meant, of course, that the affirmative action our church and society was of necessity practicing, did mean that some worthy white men – especially those white men who were in conferences, like Baltimore/Washington, with a high percentage of African/American and women clergy – would be passed over. Four years later I was a delegate to another jurisdictional conference and was privileged to campaign for my friend and colleague, Susan Morrison, who, like Forrest, was elected.

Bob helped me face the fact that I had held the high level administrative position in the conference that had helped to catapult both Forrest and Susan into the episcopacy. Hadn't it crossed my mind, he asked, that just maybe the same fate might await me? And wasn't it of some significance, he suggested, that here I was, back knocking on his door, just weeks after the 1992 jurisdictional conference had adjourned – a conference to which I had not even been elected? It took a while, but with Bob's gentle nudging I began to mourn the coming to an end, not only my life as a pastor, but also some of my dreams.

This, my final sojourn with Bob, was a wrap-up, of sorts. For both of us. He was easing his way into retirement; cutting back on the number of patients he was seeing, and scheduling fewer appointments at the office in Bethesda choosing to see more of his clients at his farm in upper Montgomery County Maryland where he raised sheep and goats. Bob guided me through retirement, and encouraged me in my second career as a speechwriter with the Federal Government. Our last hours together, he and I, both now grandfathers, both, in varying degrees, dealing with aging bodies, both persons of faith and seekers, talked a lot about issues of life and death.

Bob died just as he and I were in the process of terminating. For ten years he had been battling chronic leukemia. For most of that time, after having his spleen removed, he was in relatively good health. During the last year of his life, however, he missed more and more sessions. One day he assured me that his doctors had assured him that he would die *with* this rather than *of* it.

I remember well our last session. It was at his farm. I was on my way to the vacation home we had bought in West Virginia to play golf. He and I had been talking about my leaving therapy and on this day we decided that the next time I came would be it.

The next time I saw Bob was a couple weeks later, at his funeral. Bob's wife had called all of his patients to let us know where the services would be held. Wave and I went. His passing was celebrated in a gorgeous Orthodox chapel, The Monastery of the Holy Cross, just a few miles from Bob's farm. The priest told how Bob discovered this church. He called the bookstore where the priest was working and asked if there were any books in stock on the Jesus Prayer. The priest said yes, quite a few, and he would save one for him. He asked Bob where he lived, and when Bob told him, he said, "Why, we just opened a new church up there."

The monastery of the Holy Cross became Bob's faith home. The priest told us that Bob would come early on Sunday – often an hour before the service – and sit all alone on one of the benches along the side wall. When asked why he came so early, Bob said, "I just love this place – the symbols, the icons and the liturgy." A few days before he died, the priest told us, he went to the hospital to give Bob the sacrament of Holy Communion. When he entered the room, Bob told him he was going home. The priest said, "That's wonderful." Then Bob said, "I'm going home to my family, and then I'm going home." The priest said he must have appeared puzzled, so Bob pointed his finger heavenward and said, "I'm going home."

Looking at Bob lying in his casket, wearing a sport coat that I had seen so many times before, his beard and hair having gone from gray to white since the last time I saw him, with a small icon of the Blessed Virgin resting on his holy water soaked chest, I thought: what a fitting termination session. Ivan Ilych was Bob's very first lesson to me about death. Now he had given me his last lesson about death – his own. Bob wasn't around when I made the turn at the seventieth bend in my life. Since that was almost two years ago, perhaps Bob's last lesson took.

Chapter 10

"Admitted we were powerless over alcohol and that our lives had become unmanageable."
AA's first step

Not counting the brief sip of bourbon I took at my going away party in the meat room of Supreme Market in Boston, I took my first drink on a gorgeous fall Washington, D. C. afternoon. The Smiling Buddha Restaurant was not far from the seminary, and since it was mid afternoon, my brother, Luther, and I, and his classmate friend, Jim Bellamy, were not going there to eat. Luther and I were intent on doing something we had so longed to do. Drink.

Neither of us knew anything about alcoholism. Had we known more about its disease classification, or its tendency to revisit itself on succeeding generations, we might not have been so hell bent on ordering those glasses of wine. For us, though, this was another one of those ridiculous Nazarene taboos – like dancing and movies – that had prevented us from living the good life that we had lusted after for so long. Since we had already coughed and gagged our way through the early days of learning to smoke, now it was time to move on to bigger and better things.

One glass of wine was all I could handle. Perhaps it was guilt that made me gulp it down, like it was iced tea, or it might just have been my not knowing that alcohol was best when it was sipped. For whatever reason, my chug-a-lugging that bit of white wine sent my head into a tailspin, and for ever so brief a moment, thoughts about impending death – read God's judgment – crossed my mind.

I recovered and another glass of wine a week later went down quite nicely. And that's the way my drinking went for the next few years. A glass of wine every now and then – mostly limited to holiday dinners. And there would certainly not be any drinking done in public. Surprise of surprises, drinking alcohol for Methodists, as it had been with Nazarenes, was a taboo. Had Luther and I known that, we might have become Presbyterians. However, it was an un-enforced taboo for the laity. There was a rule in the Methodist Church Book of Discipline that forbade any drinking Methodist layperson serving on a local church's governing board, but reality had long ago moved it over to a spot next to some other no-no's from Methodism's early days, like, of all things, "the wearing of gold and costly apparel." If Luther and I had known that that exact wording was in the Discipline – wording which the Nazarene's had written into their book of rules – we most certainly would have headed for the Presbyterians.

Methodism's alcohol taboo was, however, enforced for preachers. When I met the Board of Ministerial Training and Qualification to see if they would accept me as a probationary candidate for ministry in the Methodist Church, their final order of business with me was the pledge that ministerial candidates had to sign. I was sitting up front beside John Bayley Jones, the chair of the board. It had been a relatively short interview. Members of the board asked a few theological questions, and some wanted to know not only why I was leaving the Nazarene Church, but also why I wanted to join the Methodist Church. When the questions ended, Dr. Jones, said, "Tom, there is this pledge that all candidates for the Methodist ministry have to sign. It merely asks if you are willing to abstain from the use of alcohol and tobacco in order that your witness to the faith not be compromised." I have often wondered if I would have signed that pledge. I had been so courageous, or so it seemed, when I had met with the Nazarene ministerial review board in calling them to task for what I thought were rather picayune taboos. But there was a bit of difference then: the Methodists were waiting for me with wide-open arms. Now I had nowhere else to go – my ministerial bridges had been burned behind me, and I had a wife and two small children to support. However, I never got the chance to test my courage. Dr. Jones said, "But of course, coming from the Nazarene Church, this is no problem for you." And with those words, the meeting was adjourned with my never having seen a pledge, let alone signed one.

Luther was not as fortunate. Two years later, after having finished the portion of seminary required for ordination as a probationary member, the pledge was put in front of him, and he willingly signed it. It wasn't the flat out lie that it might appear to be, for by that time, Luther and I knew that this was one of those "wink-wink, nudge-nudge" requirements – more ritual than reality – and we already had begun to compile our own list of ministerial colleagues who had signed the pledge with fingers crossed.

The periodic glass of wine continued to be the extent of my drinking life for the next three years. I did notice that on certain occasions, when the one glass would become two, I enjoyed the warm, floating sensation that I experienced. Heretofore, feelings like this had come by way of strong cough syrups, allergy medications, or, in extreme cases, the Demoral used to alleviate the pain of my repeated kidney stone attacks.

Still, I never increased the dosage of alcohol. It was a few glasses of wine scattered along the way.

A few years into my country parish days, Joe Williamson, my friend from college and seminary stopped off, with Eleanor and their two sons, to visit. Joe mixed each of us a Tom Collins, my first ever taste of the hard stuff. Here again, there was no immediate increase in my alcohol intake. Luther and Joyce were in a nearby parish and we would go out to dinner preceded with cocktails – now expanded to include daiquiris as well as highballs – but never drunken to excess.

It wasn't until we moved to St. Matthew's Church in Bowie that my drinking became more regular. This was no longer a country parish where any drinking done by Methodists was behind closed doors or with very close friends. Not so in suburban Washington. Wave and I would be invited to our church members' houses for dinner, and cocktails would be served followed by wine with the meal. One member who took me to Washington Senator baseball games introduced me to scotch, which became my drink of choice.

It was in Bowie that my drinking patterns changed. Now, it became an almost every day thing with me. Not during the day, however. Any drinking I did began after nine o'clock in the evening, which is the time I would get home after a night meeting. And for the rest of my time at Bowie that meant usually no more than a couple scotches before bed. There was some daytime drinking on Sunday afternoons if there were no meetings in the evening, and absent a night meeting, I would, on occasion, have a drink or two before dinner. Toward the end of my stay in Bowie, it was obvious that I was drinking more. I could still say that it was only two or three drinks at a time, but less and less soda and more and more scotch found their way into each of those drinks. Still in all, I was never drunk, and never missed a day of work nor an appointment.

It was at First Church Hyattsville that I started to ask my "what if" questions. What if I am an alcoholic like my Dad, or Grandpa Starnes, or Uncle Lawrence, or all those other "drunkards" whose blood flowed through my veins. The reason for the questions was that drinking was fast becoming a necessary part of my life. I looked forward to those times when I could have one or two or three. And for the first time in my life I started to sneak the drink. I began to have my two or three drinks after a night meeting, usually while watching television with Wave. Then, after turning the television off, I would take a drink into the bedroom with me. This progressed to the point where I wouldn't even pretend – Wave would kiss me goodnight, leaving me sitting there in front of the TV, drinking my way through the Tonight Show. It was also here that I began to drink myself into oblivion two, three nights a week. I still shudder when I think of how close I came to going over the edge. How many times I drove drunk, and given a congregation of 2500 members, what are the odds that over a six-year period, someone will call in the middle of the night and need a pastor. It never happened. There, but for the grace of God.

To say that this was a stressful time for me is not to say that this explains my increase in drinking. External events are never reasons for drinking. But stress was a fact of life for me. The deaths of Mama and Elizabeth and Irving and John – all in the course of a year and a half – coupled with my own health problems, served as more than just gentle reminders of my mortality. There was the financial stress of Vicky and Tommy both being in college, but at a deeper level trying also to deal with the emotional stress caused by their no longer being a part of our family's everyday life. And being the pastor of a very large church – a very diverse church, in a rapidly changing neighborhood – presented its own set of stressful challenges

By now alcohol had become my tranquilizer. I remember one evening settling into my chair in front of the television – drink by my side – feeling especially anxious, and having that anxiety start slipping away after the first few sips. No longer were my questions the "what if" ones. If I weren't an alcoholic, I felt reasonably certain that alcohol was a problem. It was impossible for me to drink just one drink. Friday evening was my favorite drinking time. The sermon would have been finished by mid-afternoon, other Sunday preparation duties would have been completed, and when Wave got home from the office, we would head to our favorite restaurant, L'escargot, on Connecticut Avenue in Washington. My intentions would always be to have just one drink, perhaps two, before dinner. But it became impossible for me to stop with just one, whatever my original intention. I usually stopped with two, though, but they would be followed with wine during the meal, and an occasional brandy with coffee after. For most normal drinkers that would be it – and for most normal drinkers even this much drinking would be considered excessive. It wasn't for me. After returning home from the restaurant, I would take my seat in front of the television, and finish off the night with a nightcap or three.

If I were not yet ready to admit that I was an alcoholic, I was long past the point of denying that I had a problem. Even though I felt that my alcohol consumption was sabotaging my therapy, perhaps even misleading the medical doctors who were trying to figure out why my erratic heartbeat was not responding to any of the medicines they were prescribing, I never raised this as an issue with either Bob Kirsch, or Dr. Loebe, my internist. One day I did tell Bob that maybe I was drinking a bit much. Since I did not tell him how much my too much was, and he didn't ask, he suggested that I limit my self to two drinks, and those two would only be consumed when Wave and I were dining out. I even began playing tricks with myself. Besides the bottle of De Wars

White Label, my favorite scotch, I would also buy a bottle of my favorite whiskey, Southern Comfort. And alternating between the two bottles – starting the night drinking scotch and finishing it off with Southern Comfort – I tried to create the illusion that I was not drinking as much simply because the level of liquid left in the bottles did not go down as fast. I did stop drinking every night, and never ever did I drink on Saturday evening. After reading an article suggesting that alcoholics drank with their left hands, I began reaching across my chest with my right hand to get the drink that was on the table beside me on the left. And strange as it seems, it came as some comfort to read of a successful person – Winston Churchill being one who comes to mind – who was known to indulge rather heavily in spirituous liquors.

Whatever games I was playing with myself, I knew better. And I reached a point when drinking was no longer fun. I could not just have one or two drinks. And even when I was enjoying the buzz that came with those first two drinks, it was a short-lived enjoyment, because I knew what the end result of the evening would be. I would pass out during a Hawaii Five-O rerun, and the next morning while emptying my liquor bottles in the kitchen sink, I would pray and ask God to forgive me, and pledge never to touch the stuff again. And I wouldn't – for that day. But the next evening, I would go by the liquor store – not the same one that I had gone to the last time, another trick of mine – and buy two more quarts of my favorites.

When I left First Church Hyattsville to become a district superintendent, my drinking did not increase in amount. I still would not drink every day, and although I now did not have to face a congregation each Sunday morning, I stayed true to my pledge not to drink on Saturday nights. Still, whenever I drank, I got drunk. Once alcohol touched my lips, there was nothing that stood between me and drunken oblivion.

It was three years into this job that I had my first blackout. I was leaving on a very early flight to Albuquerque, New Mexico. I was one of the fifty male preachers invited to attend a National United Methodist Church conference of clergy women. My drinking started on the Sunday afternoon before the flight on Monday, and when the time came to pack that evening I was rather wasted. Checking my bag at the airport the next morning, it occurred to me that I had no idea what I had packed, if anything. The night before was a total blank. I was terrified that when I got to the retreat site, there would be no clothes, and if there were clothes, none of them would match. That was not the case; I had done my usual careful selection of styles and colors.

It did scare me though, and on a bright Sunday morning, at brunch in Georgetown, I said, "I am going to stop drinking. If I can't, I am going to AA." Vicky had graduated from college and was living in the area. Tommy had just graduated from law school, but I don't know if he was there with us that afternoon. I know Vicky was, because after I made my announcement, she said, "Mom, what do you think about Dad's going to AA?" I don't remember Wave's response. My non-drinking lasted about a month, and when it resumed none of the witnesses to my grand announcement held me to it.

I had one more month long hiatus in my drinking. I remember feeling so confident in my ability to lay this burden down. I not only felt good physically, I felt good about myself. The Bishop had asked me to preach the ordination sermon at annual conference. This was quite an honor. Bishops usually kept this privilege for themselves, or invited some guest dignitary to do it for them. When I climbed up into the pulpit of the massive Cathedral of Mary Our Queen in Baltimore, I thought to myself, "Wow. Twenty five years ago, almost to the day, I came to this conference, hat in hand; now would you look at me." To celebrate, I drank that night.

But something had changed. No longer were my questions of the "what if" kind. I had long since passed that stage. Now it became more a matter of when. And my first significant when was February 1985. I had gone to the vacation home we had bought four years before in West Virginia. I would often go there by myself to play golf, and, of course, to drink. Why I went in the dead of winter, I don't remember. What I do remember is sitting on the floor in front of a fire, drinking some Vat 69 scotch – a cheaper brand, but strong enough to do the trick – and deciding that enough is enough. I put the bottle back under the kitchen sink, and never drank again that evening.

The King Singers had a new album out, which included a song, "You Are the New Day." That became my theme song. It was to me what Daddy's "Ninety and Nine" had been to him. I did feel as if I had been born again. Days of no drinking stretched into weeks and weeks stretched into months. Vicky was to be married in June, and there would be an open bar. In pricing out the affair with the caterer, it would be cheaper for us to buy the liquor. Since Tommy knew more about wines than I did, he made those selections. The wedding was a glorious event, and even with all the toasts offered, liquor never touched my lips. My new day had dawned.

However, the sun on my new day went down one November Monday evening while watching the Washington Redskins get mauled by the New York Giants – the game in which Joe Theismann, the Redskins quarterback, broke his leg. Wave was doing some paper work with a colleague of hers, and asked me to get them a glass of wine. I went down to the laundry room and got a bottle of the wine left over from Vicky's wedding. I poured them each a glass, and without giving it any thought at all, poured my self a glass. Wave and Donnie had just one glass each. Before I went to bed I drank all of what they didn't drink in that bottle, and almost all of a second one.

The next day was a meeting of the bishop's cabinet. The physical aspects of the hangover were not all that horrendous. I had had worse. But never had I had such remorse. Nine months of not drinking were gone, along with any notion of this being anything like my father's "new day." I was dean of the cabinet, sitting at the head of the table, next to the bishop – a position of leadership and prominence. I was also a drunk, plain and simple.

Living up to the slow learner label that Bob Kirsch had tacked on me, I made a couple resolutions, thinking that would do it. My two resolves were: I will not keep any liquor in the house and I will only drink when dining out. Even after nine months of sober bliss, I was not ready to admit that this was not something that Tom Starnes could handle all by himself.

I was at a new place, though. If drinking had long since ceased being fun, it was now even less fun. It was misery. For now I had those nine months of living with an unclouded mind and feeling that my life was no longer spinning out of control, looking down on me as if to say, what on earth is wrong with you, man. Never mind have you no shame; have you no sense? Still I slogged on, not drinking on as many days, but when I did pick up a drink, I still ended up drunk.

When I finished my six-year term as district superintendent, I returned to Capitol Hill, the church where I began some twenty-seven years before. I followed Ed Lewis who had returned there to stay until his retirement. It was wonderful returning where it all began. Some of the people who had been there when I came, loved to talk about those "good old days" for them, and, in some ways, even for me, when I was much thinner and had more hair. Wave and I loved walking over to Lincoln Park and reminiscing about that afternoon in 1960 when we walked round and round those park paths trying to coax Floyd into the world.

Our life in the Washington area, and our life as Methodists, seemed to have come full circle when we bought our Christmas tree at Eastern Market, the same place we bought our first one back in 1959.

Our life was good. Vicky stayed with us occasionally while taking classes at Wesley Seminary. Tommy, not yet married, had bought a house on Capitol Hill and was with a law firm in Washington. After graduating from college, Floyd was living in New York trying to make his way in the theater world. Wave was now Dr. Starnes and was the Director of the Program for Gifted and Talented in Montgomery County, Maryland. Capitol Hill was not a high maintenance church. It was a gorgeous building, with an office for me that looked out on the capitol building. The church had a magnificent organ – a transplant from the National City Presbyterian Church – acquired when that church moved from downtown to the northwest corner of the city. The congregation had decreased in size over the years, but by using a small group of young Hill staffers, little by little I increased the church's program options. I loved the worship there. The music was good, and I enjoyed having my own congregation again and each week working my way through the creative process of sermon preparation.

As less stressful as my life was, I still drank. And whenever I did, it was to excess. Not as often, though, especially around the children, because they still thought that I no longer drank. At least I think they thought that. One Friday evening I was looking forward to dinner out with Wave. The sermon was finished, Saturday was a day off, so we could go to one of our favorite Capitol Hill restaurants and I could have a drink or two. Tommy, now living on the Hill, called and asked if we wanted to go out to dinner. Knowing this meant no drinks for me, for the first time in my life, I resented sitting down and sharing a meal with one of my children. Drinking will skew your thinking; perhaps even poison your soul.

February 4th, 1987, was like most other mid-winter days in Washington, D. C., uneventful. At least I have no recollection of anything special occurring. In church we were getting ready for Ash Wednesday, the beginning of Lent. I do remember the evening very well – most of it anyway. Wave had a meeting so I decided to go out to eat. My restaurant of choice was L'Escargot, our long time favorite, up Connecticut Avenue, just north of the National Zoo. I bought a New York Times at the Peoples' Drug Store next to the restaurant, as well as a pack of cigarettes. These two items, along with the drinks I would soon order, were necessary props for the good life drama I had been acting in for some time now. All those growing up years spent in a clean and sober house, sometimes wishing that my Dad had never "found the Lord", all the while looking out on a world that seemed so much more pleasurable than the one that I was forced to live in. But those days were long since gone. Today I could sit in a smoked filled restaurant, and, with a drink in one hand and the New York Times in the other, be a part of that sophisticated world that had always eluded me.

By now the waitress knew my preferred drink: an extra dry Beefeater martini with an olive. Halfway through my term as a district superintendent, gin replaced scotch as my drug of choice. My first forays into the martini world called for a bit of Vermouth. Over the years, the amount of Vermouth lessened, until I no longer bought any. In the latter stages of my drinking life, the only things that shared space with my gin were ice cubes and olives. On that early February night, I drank two martinis, while I ate some escargots. I really wanted to put on a show. With the meal I consumed a half-liter of wine, and after the meal I downed two Grand Marnier liqueurs.

To get to our home on Capitol Hill, I had to drive south on Connecticut Avenue into downtown Washington where Connecticut becomes 17th

Street, wind my way around the Tidal Basin, and on to Independence Avenue then to Pennsylvania, and then to 4th and Pennsylvania where we lived. That is a heavily traveled route filled with stoplights and pedestrian crosswalks. I drove it drunk, and had no memory of doing so. When Wave got home, she found me sitting in front of the television with a drink by my side and that glassy eyed look that she had become so accustomed to.

Weeks before, I had seen a public service announcement on television about a program for problem drinkers at the Washington Psychiatric Institute called "New Beginnings." Wednesday morning I remembered having copied the phone number of that program. When I called, the man who answered asked me very early on in the conversation what my "drug of choice" was. That's the first time I ever considered myself a drug abuser. He and I arranged an appointment for Friday. Vicky was with us for dinner, and I told her and Wave what I had done.

Friday came and I was not the least bit apprehensive. As a matter of fact, I felt hopeful. It could have been that I thought I might be told I wasn't an alcoholic, and be introduced to a therapist who really could teach me how to drink in moderation. This idea was nixed when, in answer to my initial query – "Do you think I am an alcoholic" – the counselor answered, "Yes."

After we talked about my drinking history and my efforts at stopping, I asked him what he recommended, other than just my developing some personal discipline. He said I needed to check myself into a rehabilitation facility. I told him I couldn't possibly do that – I had a sermon to preach on Sunday morning. All right, then, he said, you have to attend ninety meetings of Alcoholics Anonymous in ninety days. There's no way I can do that, I countered. I am a very busy man. I knew he had given all the slack he was going to give, when he said, "You weren't too busy to find time to drink." He then took out a small pamphlet, titled "Where and When" that listed all the AA meetings in the greater Washington area. He circled one and told me that it would be a good fit for me. It was in Old Town Alexandria, just across the Potomac, a short drive from Capitol Hill. "It meets at noon," he said. "It's a good meeting and you probably won't run into any of your members." He then said, "Right now this might appear to be the worst day of your life. Trust me. It isn't. You will look back on this day as one of your best. Let me tell you something else. You are going to find catacomb Christianity at its best in all those church basements you are going to be entering in the next ninety days."

So, the next Tuesday, February 11, one week after my last drink, I circled Christ Church, Episcopal, in the center of Old Town, three times before I parked the car. My heart was pounding as I entered the parish house and walked down into the basement room that would come to be for me what that little Nazarene Church in Cowan, Tennessee had been for my Dad. There were classroom tables pushed together in the center of the room surrounded by chairs. There were also chairs pushed back against the walls on each side. I took one of the chairs along the wall. Julie was leading the meeting. She read a preamble – a sort of an AA mission statement – taken from something called a "Big Book." Julie said that she was celebrating seven months of sobriety. Everybody applauded.

At 12:30, Julie announced that it was half time. She said something about AA not having any dues or fees, and somebody picked up a little breadbasket from a side table and passed it around and everyone put in a dollar. She then said, "Is this anyone's first AA meeting?" My heart was in my throat as I raised my hand. She asked if I would like to identify myself, I nodded, and said, "I'm Tom and I'm an alcoholic." Tears came to my eyes but not enough to keep me from seeing Elizabeth and David bow their heads and move their lips. They were saying a prayer for me. When I left the meeting, Julie and Steve handed me a little scrap of paper on which each of them had written their phone numbers. I carry that slip of paper – now laminated – in my wallet, along with a small copy of the promises of AA – also laminated – that Ralph gave me.

From that winter day almost twenty years ago, not only have I not taken a drink, I have never wanted to. I am one of the lucky ones. The compulsion that had dogged me for so long vanished. It is still just one day at a time, I know that, and as I have heard so often, and from the bottom of my heart believe, I am just one drink away from a drunk.

What has AA to do with my faith journey? It certainly didn't enrich my ministry that much since I was but seven years away from retirement when I finally put the bottle down. And strange as it might seem, during some of my most tormented years I did some of my best preaching. When I go back and read those words of mine that were written on some of my darkest days, all I can say is that I spoke better than I knew, and when it came to faith and trust – which I preached about a lot – I was making "the wish the father of the thought." I so wanted the faith and trust of my preaching to be mine.

AA did cause me to see for the first time the truth of that old hymn I grew up with, "All to Jesus I Surrender." How often did we sing that around the altar, after a service, when folks had come forward – folks that usually included me – to find the peace in their hearts, that, we were told, the world could not possibly give. AA taught me what full surrender meant. In the program we refer to it as "turning it over." It's an admission of weakness. It's saying, "I can't do this by myself. I need help." And we reach out to a Higher Power – in my case God – and let our care rest in his care. In AA, it's not good form to try and figure how it all works. "Don't play head games. That's what got you here." You hear that a lot in the "rooms." I have concluded that, for me at least, and I think for most others, this "turning it over" is the closest one can come to knowing how it works. It's all that I did differently. Therapists, self-control, books, prayer, even shame, didn't do it. It was only when I raised my hand, admitting I was powerless, and throwing myself on the mercy of a Higher Power and a room full of drunks, that I was delivered from this particular demon.

Prayer and God have become more real to me through meeting in those basement rooms. A lot of the people, who gather there three, four, five times a week, aren't church people. A fair number of them haven't the nicest things to say about organized religion. And yet most of the ones I have met believe that God is with them, and that if all they do "is the next right thing," everything's going to be all right. Not perfect, mind you. They know better than that. Maybe not the way they would wish it to be. But it will be okay now that they have a Higher Power looking out for them. And most all of these "spiritual pagans," as my friend Gerry calls them, he being one of them, gets down on their knees – literally – each day, and commits that day to the care of God.

I have also met so much personal triumph in "these rooms." Jeffry was in that Christ Church group where I started. He has difficulty speaking, and walks with a noticeable limp. He had every reason to drink, but that wouldn't help, he would say, now would it. So he kept at it, and once, years later after I had moved away, I returned to the group. Jeffry was there, still sober, now married, and he had brought his three-year-old child to the meeting with him. I remember a Naval Academy graduate, who lost everything: business, wife, house, and had to start over in his mid-life years. But he was making it, and was, for the first time in his life, living out one of AA's favorite aphorisms, "happy, joyous, and free." There was a professional, lawyer I think, who would crawl into his car trunk, out of sight of his wife, and drink. In AA sad stories were, more often than not, told with grace and sometimes humor. One well-respected businessman lost everything, and to describe his financial "bottom", said his credit was so bad that he was denied admission to the Book-Of-The-Month Club.

Again, it came a bit late, but AA did give me a glimpse of what Jesus might have had in mind for his followers. Remember that first meeting and my noticing Elizabeth and David praying for me. That didn't end that group's interest in me. Old stuttering Ralph, who wore garish hats, kept me supplied with literature. He gave me my first list of the AA promises, as well as the full copy of Reinhold Niebuhr's serenity prayer. He also gave me a small copy of the Big Book, AA's Bible. It has a dark blackish/blue cover, and the title is embossed, making it unreadable from any distance. When he gave it to me, he said, "It l-l-looks l-l-like a B-b-bible so your parishioners w-w-w-ill never know." The group also asked me to serve as secretary for a few months. AA secretaries don't take minutes. Their only duty is to take care of the money collected at the meetings. It was the group's way of holding on to me.

I did make the ninety meetings in ninety days, which meant that some days I would double up, and, on some weekends, triple up. On the first Saturday of my AA life, I went to a meeting in Herndon, Virginia. Herndon was one of those small rural communities that were being engulfed in the greater Washington suburban sprawl. Spotting the gun rack sporting pickup trucks, as well as a few Harleys, parked around the building, it occurred to me that this group just might bear little resemblance to the Christ Church group that consisted mostly of people who looked like me.

The men inside were dressed in jeans, not at all uncommon for Saturday mornings even in upscale suburban communities, but there are jeans and there are jeans. And these jeans were the kind that needed a big buckled belt. And the faces of these men who wore these big buckled belted jeans showed signs of wear and tear. They greeted each other, sharing bits of information – information that I noticed contained a few more "fucks" and "goddamns" than I had heard at the pre-meeting sharing at Christ Church. Neil opened the meeting with the preamble, and then, like Julie, asked if anyone was here for the first time. I said, "I'm Tom, and I'm an alcoholic. This is my first time at this meeting." They gave the usual, "Hi, Tom," and then added, "Keep coming back." Neil told a bit of his story then asked if anyone else wanted to share. Someone told a bit of their story, and then a young man – thin, not more than early twenties – started to share his story that concerned his inability to shake his compulsion "to use" – a term reserved for those who are addicted to narcotics. Neil interrupted him, mid sentence, telling him that this was an AA meeting; if he had a fucking problem with cocaine, he needed to get his ass to an NA meeting; we are here today to talk about drinking not drugging. I was stunned. I needed to share, and I wanted to share, but Neil had put the fear of God into me. At length I raised my hand, and again said that I was Tom and an alcoholic, and they again said, Hi Tom. I told them that I was new to the program, that this was just my fifth meeting, and that I was already grateful for AA and so glad that it had been there to help me, because nothing else had seemed to work for me.

It was a rough, tough, group. Or so it seemed. I felt so out of place. But when I started to leave, Neil came over to me, shook my hand, gave me a book, and told me to "keep coming back." The book, <u>Living Sober</u>, is a well known staple of recovery groups, and on the inside of the cover every person present that day had not only signed his name but given me his phone number as well. That book is among my treasures; not for its content – you can find what it says in any number of other books

– but for its reminder to me of those fellow strugglers who were there for me in the beginning, and have been there for me all along the way. I could not have made it without them.

On the next day, Sunday, Wave and I were leaving after church to spend a few days at our house in West Virginia. I had marked an early afternoon meeting that I could attend along the way. Wave had brought the Washington Post to read in the car while I did my recovery work. It seemed strange when we pulled up that people were leaving. I went inside anyway, and a few men were still lingering with their cups of coffee. They apologized for the wrong time still appearing in the "Where and When" – it takes awhile to get these changes made, they said. One of them asked me how long I had, and when I said, twelve days, he looked over at his two buddies and said, "This guy needs a meeting." Then the three of them sat back down, listened to a bit of my story, told me a bit of theirs, and then sent me on my way with the Serenity Prayer and the Lord's Prayer, followed by AA's closing admonition, "Keep coming back."

And that's how it has been for these almost twenty years. Groups – all kinds of groups – meeting in all kinds of places – mostly church basements – with one thing in common: one drunk helping another drunk by sharing each other's "experience, strength and hope."

AA saved my life. In my first year of sobriety, I lost forty pounds, and, over time, Dr. Loebe weaned me off the medicine he had been prescribing for my irregular heartbeats. Alcohol was not just medicating me; it was killing me.

AA also helped make the faith I had, in hope, been preaching, more real to me. It showed me that peoples' lives could be turned around. All those scripture verses I had heard about "old things passing away and all things becoming new", I witnessed; not just in others, but also in me. I even came to believe that Mama's plaque on the wall that looked down on me in my growing up years – the one that pictured Jesus praying in the garden along with those three promising words that I had always hoped were true, but wondered about, "Prayer changes things" – were in fact true. Stories I have consistently heard told in AA rooms about people getting down on their knees, asking God to help them and that requested help coming. I have seen people reach out to each other – people with nothing more in common than a desire to stay sober – and just by linking arms, have managed to make it through, one day at a time. For years I sang,

> "Blest be the ties that bind, our hearts in Christian Love,
>
> The fellowship of kindred minds is like to that above.
>
> We share each other's woes, each other's burdens bear,
>
> And for each other flows the sympathizing tear."

It was AA that showed me that this hope of the blessed community – a hope that Jesus no doubt had for those who would follow him – could in fact become reality, if only the church could, to put it in Big Book jargon, "learn to practice these principles in all its affairs." It was AA that cleared up for me, once and for all, what it means to have faith. Faith is not mental assent. Faith, Jesus style, is more heart than head. "The Devils in Hell believe," he said once. Faith for our Lord was trust. "Casting all our care upon Him." "Resting in the Lord." It remained for AA to give me a better phrase for faith – one that suited me, and I think, is still true to the gospel's meaning: turning it over.

About 18 months into sobriety, the bishop asked me to come and be his program director. I loved Capitol Hill Church – loved living on the hill

– but I still had this commitment of mine to be true to Methodism's appointment process. The job did sound interesting, so I agreed to do it. However, the job and I were not a good fit. I didn't preach often, but one of the Sundays that I did, a man, on his way out, shook my hand and told me that I should be doing that every Sunday. Given my resurrected belief that God does, sometimes, speak through others, and Vicky's telling me that she was tired of hearing me complain about my job; that I should do as I had so often told my children to do, "Either shit or get off the pot," I told my bishop that I wanted a church. I also told him – I know he didn't understand it – that now since I really had something to preach, with conviction, that it was foolish for me not to have a place where I could do it, week in and week out.

I had always loved these words from Job's concluding conversation with God, "I had heard of thee by the hearing of the ear, but now my eye sees thee." Now I loved them even more. So much of what I had preached and hoped for over the years had been, as Job put it, "by the hearing of the ear." It was Alcoholics Anonymous that helped me see it.

Chapter 11

"Preach faith until you have it, and then because you have it, you will preach it."

Peter Boehler, to John Wesley

Philips Brooks defined preaching as "truth communicated through personality." While I am not ready to apply the "truth" part of this definition to my preaching, I will, however, lay claim to the "personality" part. Preaching, for me, has been a decidedly personal faith quest. It didn't start out to be that. For whatever reason – maybe it was in fact a "call from God" – I decided to make the ministry my life's work, and being a preacher meant preaching sermons. And from the outset preaching was the focus of my ministerial life. Whenever possible, the major portion of each day was set aside for reading, brooding over the selected subject, gathering supportive materials, and writing. The other things preachers have to do – visit the sick, attend committee meetings, manage the church's business, counsel – were given spots in my daily "to do" list, but preaching always took precedence.

In the beginning, though, preaching was just one of those things clergy were supposed to do: important, as well as necessary, but little more than part of the job description. Over time, however, preaching became the main thoroughfare on my journey of faith.

It never occurred to me that this was the case. It didn't even enter my mind a few years ago when we were packing for our move to Rehoboth Beach. After retiring from the parish ministry, all my sermon manuscripts were stored in boxes. Years ago my son Tommy ordered me to not throw any of them away. So every sermon I have ever preached – most of them in long hand, on yellow legal pads, starting with those preached to my eighteen members in Easton – were in those boxes. I wanted to put them in more durable file cartons for the move, and also arrange them in some sort of alphabetical order – alphabetical by general subject matter. While I was reaching into those old boxes and pulling out files, I noticed that some folders contained only two or three sermons, whereas others were bulging with manuscripts. I knew I had favorite topics, but not to this extent.

Noting the five bulging files – Faith and Doubt, Life and Living, the Church, Suffering, Social Issues – didn't even suggest to me that during all those years preaching had been, primarily, a faith construction project for me. It was my preacher daughter, Vicky, who turned my head in this direction.

I was telling her about my writing – listing the areas I wanted to cover – my father's conversion, college days, seminary, leaving the Nazarene Church, therapy, AA, seminary, etc. – and she said, "Dad, you have to devote a section to preaching. That's played such a significant part in your faith journey." And I remembered one of my emails to my friend Herb Dodge who had asked me to share with him what I had been preaching for these almost fifty years since both of us said goodbye to the Nazarene Church. In that email – included in the introduction to this book – I suggested that perhaps I have been "trying to find my own way by preaching it out."

Through Fear to Faith

When I finished tapping out the line you have just finished reading, I shut down the laptop, having struggled my way through just a couple pages worth of writing. It just wasn't clear what I was trying to say about this preaching-as-autobiography style of mine. The final segment of the Jim Lehrer News Hour that evening was an interview with Kate Di Camillo, who had just been awarded a Newberry Medal for her recently published children's book, <u>The Tale of Despereaux</u>. The interviewer commented that all of his children – from the youngest to the oldest – loved her books. How do you explain this, he asked? How do you write a book that will have an appeal to children of all ages? Just who is your audience? Ms. Di Camillo paused, and then said, "My audience is me." That's it, I thought. The audience I have been preaching to for all these years has been me.

This explains those five bulging sermon files stored away with all those other not so bulging sermon files waiting for Tommy to decide if he feels the same way now as he did on that day long ago when he ordered me not to throw any one of them away. But, whatever happens to those old sermons is really of no consequence to me. They had their day. There were those special times when someone would tell me that a sermon had been helpful; had given them a new way of looking at an old truth, perhaps, or, maybe, just enough hope for them to believe that tomorrow was going to be a bit better than today. And I really did want to preach to my congregations' needs. But my primary audience had all along, I suppose, been me.

Take the monster file labeled "Faith and Doubt." Coming to terms with my own beliefs and disbeliefs has been a life long struggle. Maybe Brother Boggs, our first Nazarene pastor in Delaware, was on to something when, with a twinkle in his eyes, he would call this little four year old "Doubting Thomas."

It was questioning and doubting that had made my move to the Methodist Church a necessity. Still in all, even I wasn't sure. So those early sermons were attempts to legitimize doubt. I must have felt that doubt had to have a place in faith because of the label I tacked on to the file: "Faith and Doubt." Early on I made them blood brothers.

I remember discovering a sermon that Harry Emerson Fosdick had preached to his Riverside Church congregation in New York, City, titled, "Doubting Your Doubts." His point being, don't run from your doubts; face them squarely until you can begin to doubt even your doubts. Fosdick was engaged in a running battle with the fundamentalists of his day – making a place for a liberal interpretation of Scripture – and I read whatever of his I could get my hands on. And more than just a few of his lines made their way into my sermons. I read a lot of Leslie Weatherhead in these early days, too. He was the London preacher whose book, <u>When the Lamp Flickers</u>, had such a profound influence on me in seminary. So when his new book, <u>The Christian Agnostic</u>, was published, I devoured it. More than one of my sermons in those early years had this borrowed quote in it: "There is a thread of agnosticism that runs throughout the scriptures."

Preaching to myself didn't stop me from addressing someone else's needs I soon discovered. Hazel McCann lived across the road from the North Harford parsonage. She owned and operated the general store up at the crossroads which was downtown Dublin. Her husband, Lamar, had run the family business for years. It became her responsibility one Saturday afternoon after he walked down behind the barn out back and put a gun to his head. Lamar had for years been "seeing" another woman, and rumor had it that she had either had enough of him or found someone else. Mrs. McCann held her head high, as we used to say, and made her way alone. She watched over the young preacher and his family – baking donuts and being on call when some spur of the moment happening – usually a trip to the doctor by either a parent or a child – made a sitter's presence necessary. Leaving church one Sunday morning, she didn't offer up the usual, "nice sermon." What she did was thank me for suggesting that doubt was a part of any faith worth having, and confessing that for years she had struggled with faith questions, all the while feeling that because of her doubts, this meant that she was not a true Christian.

Bill Walker was another member of that northern Maryland congregation. Actually, he wasn't a member when I came as pastor. He was a free spirit, a bit eccentric with a marvelous sense of humor. He drove an MG and had his clothes tailored with fabrics shipped from Scotland. Rings were wrapped around multiple fingers, and it was nothing to see him drape a fur cape over his shoulders. But even in this conservative rural town, Bill was accepted, loved and appreciated. He assumed sole care for his mother and was with her through her later years of dementia.

Although Bill sang in the choir and was responsible for the altar flowers, he had never joined the church. He, like Mrs. McCann, had a questioning mind, and when I gave him permission to keep his doubts even as he confirmed his faith, he made his own profession. Bill has been a life long friend, a guest at all our family's rites of passage, and will be there in a month or so when Wave and I celebrate our fifty years together.

Tucked in that bulging faith and doubt file are sermons preached when I questioned whether I had any faith at all. Those were the days when I was traveling down to Dr. Finn's office on Read Street in Baltimore. It was during this time that I discovered St. John of the Cross, and learned a new phrase, "dark night of the soul." Harry Emerson Fosdick's writings gave way to Frederick Robertson's sermons – a nineteenth century pulpit master – and on one of my darker days, I read how he experienced his own dark night of the soul, and my eyes fixed on these words of his:

> "In the darkest hours through which a human soul can pass, whatever else is doubtful, this, at least, is certain. If there be no God, and no future state, yet, even then, it is better to be generous than selfish, better to be chaste than licentious, better to be true than false, better to be brave than to be a coward."

How I clung to those words, as well as to the hope that even if the phrase I heard so often, "this, too, shall pass," was not Biblical, it could very well be true.

Having to preach each week – just having to show up – kept me at it, which, for me, meant reading. And that meant mining such treasures as Walter Russell Bowie telling me that "God may speak better through his absences," or Ernest Hemingway assuring me that when his writing hit a rough spot, he needed to remember that all he really had to do was write one true sentence.

As the years passed, making a case for doubting occupied fewer and fewer lines in my sermons. I would hit it now and then – usually if the lectionary reading suggested it as a topic, or, if not a topic, a point in a sermon. I remember toward the end of my preaching days, I read Eric Sevareid's last news commentary when he retired from CBS. He listed a few of the rules that he imposed upon himself as he attempted to comment on the news of the day. Here's the last one from that list: "To retain the courage of one's doubts as well as one's convictions in this world of dangerously passionate certainties."

By now, I had reached the stage where faith and doubt belonged together. In my heart at least, they were joined at the hip. I often quoted Reinhold Niebuhr, a twentieth century theologian, who said that there was a time in his life when he had all the answers, but his "real growth began when (he) discovered that the questions to which (he) had the answers were not the important questions." If I included this line in a sermon, I would usually follow it with Elie Wiesel's similar comment: "Most good questions remain unanswered." About this time I picked up a book by a little known writer and came across these words: "mystery is an authentic category of existence." I no longer have the book, and since I do not even remember the author I can't check the quote. What I do remember is the essence of the chapter: mystery is not unanswered questions, and given enough time and enough smarts it can be done away with. Not at all. Mystery is an authentic category of existence. It just is. As the apostle Paul said, "Behold, I show you a mystery."

Frederich Buechner soon made his way into my life. I don't remember the first book of his I read, but by now I have read all of his non-fiction. He made faith and doubt all of a piece. "Faith is a way of seeing in the dark." How I have treasured that line. And these words as well:

> "In my own experience, the ways God appears in our lives are elusive and ambiguous always. There is always room for doubt in order, perhaps, that there will always be room to breathe. There is so much in life that hides God and denies the very possibility of God that there are times when it is hard not to deny God altogether. Yet it is possible to have faith nonetheless. Faith *is* that nonetheless."

Even during this time of focusing on faith as belief, and making a place for doubt, another faith note began to be sounded in my sermons: faith defined as trust. I had first heard this in my seminary days. There I learned that in the New Testament two Greek words were used for faith: *ascensus* and *fiducia*. *Ascensus* was used to define faith as belief, and *fiducia* was used to define faith as trust. This faith as trust got some airtime in my early years of preaching – a mention here and there. However, it was in the middle years of my life, the time the Psalmist may have been referring to when he talked about "the destruction that wasteth at noonday," that faith as trust was the only kind of faith I preached about. In these times when my life seemed to be spiraling out of control, more than once I would tell myself, through my listeners, about the day that Frederick Buechner, trying to navigate his own troubled waters, spied a vanity license plate that said simply, "Trust." He guessed, correctly as it later turned out, that the car belonged to some bank employee, but that didn't matter. To him it was a sign. I remember reading, and then preaching, that some ancient writers in the church defined faith as "falling into God," which is just another way of putting the phrase I was raised on, "rest in the Lord." And, of course, it was in the rooms of AA that I came to believe what I was preaching about faith as trust. In "the program" it's called "turning it over." It was only when I gave up trying to stop drinking, on my own, and turned it over to my higher power, that, not only was the dreaded compulsion to drink lifted, but now I could preach, with conviction, the life transforming power of faith as "falling into God," or "resting in the Lord," or simply, "turning it over."

Almost as big as my "faith and doubt" file is the one tabbed, "Life and Living." This was my catchall folder – filled with sermons on a variety of everyday situations. Again, it reflected my own need to make sense of what was going on in the world around me. Years later, the wisdom in my spending so much Sunday morning time on day-in-day-out issues was ratified in a poll that found that a significant motivating factor in getting people into a church pew on Sunday morning is the hope that they will get some direction on how to make it through the next week.

There are sermons here from those dark nights of my soul that bear rather ominous titles – suggesting a depth of depression that I do not remember feeling: "Is Life Worth Living" and "Life Without Purpose." Vicky came reeling into the living room of our Capitol Hill parsonage one night, crying and announcing that "the house is broken, the house is broken." She and Tommy had been playing "ring around the rosy" and she was dizzy. I used her experience to preach a sermon titled, "It's All in the Way You Look at It," suggesting that, as Anais Nin put it, we don't necessarily see things as they are. Rather, we see things as we are.

There are not a lot of sermons from my North Harford days in this file. Life and Living sermons began in earnest with the move to Bowie. There I talked a lot about marriage and family issues. These were the middle sixties and the nuclear family was under siege; some even suggesting that it was on its way out. Divorce rates were climbing. Children were running away from home, or being tossed out – boys especially – in some instances just for having long hair. Burl Ives was telling us that "the times they are a changing" and the Beattles were showing us that this was indeed the case.

Entering mid life at Bowie, and continuing into my years at First Church, Hyattsville, I tried to preach my way through that turbulent time of life, with such titles as "Hang in There" and "A Man For All Seasons." One Sunday when the Gospel lesson was the story of the woman who washed Jesus' feet with a bottle of expensive perfume, and Jesus told his disciples to cool it when they fussed about "such waste", I preached to that upwardly mobile, high achieving suburban congregation a sermon that I titled, "For No Good Reason." In it I quoted a poem that became a favorite:

> "If of thy mortal goods, thou art bereft,
>
> > And from thy meager store two loaves alone to thee are left,

> Sell one, and with the dole,
>
> Buy hyacinths to feed thy soul."

When Tommy left college after his second year, and headed to the Maine woods to make his way, I read some Thoreau – about his retreat to Walden woods – and preached a sermon that I labeled, "Simplify, Simplify."

Looking over this file leaves little doubt that my audience was me. In 1979, when the last child had left home for college, my drinking had reached critical levels, I was in therapy with Bob Kirsch, and I had suffered what at least one doctor thought was a mini-stroke, I preached on "Made for Bigger Things." The lesson that morning was from my favorite chapter in the Bible, Romans 8. Paul says, as least we think it is Paul who said it,

> "For in this hope we were saved. Now hope that is seen is not hope. For who hopes for what he sees? But if we hope for what we do not see, we wait for it with patience."

I opened the sermon with a quote from Nikos Kazantzakis: "Every woman has a wound that will not heal." Wave and I had just seen Lorraine Hansberry's play, "The Sign in Sidney Brustein's Window". Sidney's little newspaper is on the skids, he has an ulcer, his wife has left him and his sister has committed suicide. And a friend is calling him a fool for not giving up. Here's the line from that play that I read to my congregation:

> "Always have been. A fool that believes that death is waste, and love is sweet and that the earth turns and men change every day and that rivers run and that people wanna be better than they are."

I followed this with a paragraph from Henri Nouwen's, The Wounded Healer. Then, speaking directly to the turbulence within me, I said to that July Sunday congregation,

> "Well, there are the quotes. A novelist who says we all have a wound that won't heal. A playwright who has a beaten down man still get up and say that people "wanna" be better than they are. And a priest who says that our problem is we think we can heal this wound with the right woman, or the right man, or the right job, and we think that what we need to make us better is out there somewhere, if only we could find it and then have it."

A decided shift occurred in my Life and Living preaching when I moved into my senior years. Once again affirming that my audience was indeed me, I began to preach occasionally about the inner life, especially prayer. In my earlier years, I don't think I ever preached a sermon dedicated wholly to the subject of prayer. The reason being, I suppose, that I did very little of it. Except, of course, the kind of public praying which preachers get paid to do. Having grown up in a family, and a church, where "saying one's prayers" was a Christian duty, perhaps I too closely identified prayer with the Nazarene Church holy life style. The guilt I felt about not being a "man of prayer" was assuaged, somewhat, when Bishop Robinson published his little book, <u>Honest to God</u>, in the early sixties. He never prayed, he wrote, in the commonly understood ways. Praying for him was engaging in deep thought, or having a serious conversation with another person.

However, when my life began to unravel in that "destruction that wasteth at noonday" period, Bishop Robinson's prayer as deep thought or serious conversation just wasn't enough. So I began to pray, in the way I had been taught as a boy, simply asking God to please help me. I started praying for my children as they were moving out trying to find their way in the world, like my Dad had prayed for all of his children every morning before he headed out to grind out his eight hours standing in front of the giant lathe he operated in du Pont's machine shop. And even though my head has never let me believe that prayer could physically heal anyone, my heart led me to stand by grandson Jacob in the emergency room at Children's Hospital, his little body wired up as if he were heading out on a space mission, struggling for its next breath, and ask God to please make him well.

Frederich Buechner replaced Bishop Robinson as my tutor on prayer. In <u>Now and Then</u> he tells of going to hear Agnes Sanford lecture on prayer. Praying was not something that he had done in anything approaching a regular manner. But he decided to give it a try. This is how he writes of that experience:

> "Every morning before school began, I would bicycle up Tan Lane to the school church, and there, in that shabby old building – all by myself with breakfast coffee still warm in my stomach and trying to empty my mind of the thousand things I would have to start doing when the bell rang for classes – I would kneel in one of the creaking, varnished pews and pray simply for the power to pray, … Did they work, those early morning prayers with breakfast on my breath? How can you ever be sure? How can you know what you would have been, what you would have done, if you hadn't prayed? … I can only say that I kept on doing it week after week and to a lesser degree, more haphazardly, dimly, without the bicycle, have kept on doing it ever since."

So whenever the lectionary suggested it, I would preach on prayer – not trying to prove its validity, or hold it up as required Christian behavior – but rather as part of our paying attention to the needs of the heart. Prayer as soul food, you could say. My final ministerial years' reading consisted mostly of books on the inner life. I did a ten-day silent retreat at a Jesuit retreat center in Gloucester, Massachusetts, during my last pastorate. While there, I listened to some Thomas Merton tapes. Although I had known of him – was even acquainted with some of his thinking – I had never read any of his writings. His books, along with those of Thomas More, Gerald May and Henri Nouwen became my main sources for most of my sermons on life and living during those final years of preaching.

Another of my big files is simply marked "Church." And looking over the titles suggests the same trajectory that I found in the previous two that I have mentioned, Faith and Doubt, and Life and Living. A trajectory, you could say, from the head to the heart.

For instance in my early preaching days sermons on the church were attempts to make a case for the church. Just why are we here – we people of God? What is our reason to be, or, to put it in church talk, what is our mission? I remember telling on more than one occasion the story that I have long since forgotten where I read it – even whether or not it is true – about an Indian Prince, grieving over the death of his wife, who commissioned an artisan to sculpt an exquisite alabaster tomb in her memory. Over the years as more and more tourists came the prince had a large pavilion built over the tomb. The crowds increased necessitating an even larger mausoleum. That work of art, with its massive marble central chamber, became one of the wonders of the world. One day, as the prince was looking down from one of the high galleries, something didn't look right. There was an object on the floor, right in the middle of that beautifully crafted room, that didn't seem to fit. So he called in the artisan once more, and ordered them to remove that object – the object being his wife's tomb – which was, after all, the reason for the building in the first place.

I preached that theme a lot in those early and middle years. I used the Ezekial "dry bones" story a few times, asking whether even God Almighty could breathe new life into these old bones we call the church. I chastised my congregations, especially in the sixties and seventies, for not taking its rightful place alongside all those who were marching on behalf of peace and justice for all. Picking up on something I read in the newspapers about a mother suing the school system for failing in its attempts to educate her son, I preached a sermon that I titled, "Taking the Church to Court."

As the years piled up, though, my preaching on the subject of church took on a different character. I would still get after the folks on occasion, but my chiding them usually had to do with them not being the beloved community that I was certain our Lord had in mind for us to be. When "passing the peace" made its way into protestant worship, and I began to make a place for it in the service, cries of horror went up about this intrusive bit of glad handing that was destroying the solemnity of everyone's trying to be still and know that God is God. This was the time when the phone company was telling us "to reach out and touch someone" so I tacked that title onto a sermon of mine. In that sermon, I asked what could be more intrusive than to have about six or eight men (ushers were mostly men when I preached this sermon) shove plates full of money in our faces about half way through those times when we were trying "to be still and know." I also reminded them that worship was not our "one-on-one" times with God. Worship was a communal experience, and the "passing of the peace" was the church's way of saying that we are here together as a community of faith. After my experience with AA, on more than one occasion, I preached on the "Upstairs/Downstairs" ways of being the church. In these later years I would talk about the 12 Step recovery groups that were meeting in our church basements and not talking community, as those of us upstairs were consistently doing, but actually living it. The church, I wound up saying toward the end, whenever I preached on the subject, ought to be like the home Robert Frost described in his "The Death of the Hired Man,"

"Home is the place where, when you go there, they have to take you in."

Remember the poll I mentioned previously that sought to determine why people went to church? Three reasons were given. The one I mentioned was to see if they might hear some word on how to help them make it through the days of their lives. The only other one of the three responses I remember, I call the "Cheers" answer. That's the name of the television series loosely based on a bar in Boston – a place where everybody knows your name. That's what the people polled said they wanted from a church. They wanted a community in which they could find a place; a place where, maybe not everybody there, but most everybody there, anyway, might know their name.

Bulging file number four contains attempts of mine to deal with life's troubles and sorrows. Unlike the other three I have mentioned, there is no traveling from the head to the heart in this one. If there is a trajectory at all, it has to do with quality of writing. I was saying the same thing about suffering when my preaching days ended that I was saying when they began.

And from the outset I saw suffering as one of life's givens. "The rain falls on the just and the unjust." It never occurred to me to trace its trail back to the hand of God. I had certainly heard it preached, even heard it suggested to families grieving the loss of a child, such drivel as "God must have wanted a songbird in heaven so he took your little darling away." I never believed this. How could I – growing up in a family with a brother who spent the last twelve years of his life in bed, crippled with muscular dystrophy, and died gasping for his last breath at twenty-seven. What this young man could have become and achieved, had he been given a shot at his three score and ten. A few months in the first grade, and a visit or two by a home tutor was all the formal education he ever received. But with the assistance of his ever-present Bible and Life magazine, he taught himself to read, and the dial on his radio opened up to him the world out there. Science says that Luther and I should have shared Benton's fate. The strain of muscular dystrophy in our family is carried by the women and affects all male children. Before we knew this, my sister Lucille gave birth to a son, David, whose gift of life was just three more years than Benton's. Never for a moment did it cross my mind that God picks and chooses those who will suffer. And that somehow, for reasons known only to him, decided to spare Luther and me.

So, I started out preaching a very simple gospel of suffering whose first point got encapsulated years later in a bumper sticker: "shit happens." Suffering just is, I would preach, and our task – yours and mine – is to make the most of it. I was forever putting my spin on Romans 8, making Paul say, "all things *can* work together for some good." It's up to us. It all depends on what we decide to do with the trouble that is sure to come.

One of my early sermons on suffering and trouble was titled "Wells in the Valleys." The text for that sermon was a little known – at least to me – line in the 84th Psalm, "Passing through the valley of Baca, they make it a well." The Hebrew word for Baca is related to a verb that means "to weep" or "to cry." It was given this name because the trees there gave off globules of gum that resembled tears. So I preached that when we are passing through our valleys of tears, maybe we ought to try digging some wells. I found a bit of doggerel to quote. It was a poem about two frogs that fell into a can of milk. One of them, noticing the "shiny and steep" inner sides of that milk can, gave up any hope of survival.

> "But number Two, of sterner stuff,
>
> Dog-paddled in surprise,
>
> The while he wiped his milky face
>
> And dried his milky eyes.
>
> 'I'll swim awhile, at least,' he said –
>
> Or so I've heard he said.
>
> 'It really wouldn't help the world
>
> If one more frog were dead'
>
> An hour or two he kicked and swam,
>
> Not once he stopped to mutter,
>
> But kicked and kicked and swam and kicked –
>
> Then hopped out, via butter."

Those country churches of mine loved that foolish bit of verse. I, having minored in literature in college, set this bit of doggerel aside when I moved to suburban Washington, feeling that it really didn't do justice to my more refined poetic tastes. However, in the early seventies, I read Claude Brown's bestseller, <u>Manchild in the Promised Land</u>. While still a boy, Claude Brown was hooked on heroin, been shot, and earned a police record. By all accounts his was a lost cause. You know what turned this man-child around? A mentor who saw promise in this boy, and, for God knows whatever reason – it might have been the only poem he knew – quoted Claude Brown that silly poem about the two frogs that fell into a can of milk – the same poem that I felt didn't meet my literary standards – and Claude Brown decided not to go down without a fight.

My trouble and suffering sermons, like most of my other sermons – especially in the early and middle years – had three points. Point number one was that trouble is a fact of life. Some get more. Some get less. But as the old saying goes, "there is no home on earth that will not, someday, have its hush." My second point was the one about "digging wells" or kicking your way out of a milk can. But, for me at least, and, I think, in order to be true to the Christian gospel, there had to be a third point: we are not alone in this struggle of ours to overcome. God is with us – all the way.

I preached a sermon that I titled, "I Never Promised You a Rose Garden." In church the previous Sunday morning, my son Floyd and his friend, Ellen LePore, sang a song that I had sung so often back in my Nazarene days.

> "God hath not promised skies always blue,
>
> Flower strewn pathways all our lives through.
>
> God hath not promised sun without rain,
>
> Joy without sorrow, peace without pain.
>
> God hath not promised we shall not know,
>
> Toil and temptation, trouble and woe,
>
> He hath not told us we shall not bear many a burden many a care.

> "But God hath promised strength for the day,
>
> Rest for the labor, light for the way.
>
> Grace for the trials, help from above,
>
> Unfailing kindness, undying love."

So in that sermon I repeated to the congregation what Floyd and Ellen had sung the previous week. No, we have not been promised a rose garden. Yes, troubles come. But we are not in this alone. God has promised us grace and strength and undying love.

You see, I had to add this third point, simply because I wasn't far along in this preaching life of mine before I discovered, if I didn't already know it, that there are some valleys where you will dig long and hard, and still not get any water, and some milk cans you may fall into will be just too deep and too slippery for you to ever kick your way out of. Then, all any of us can rest on is the assurance that a power greater than ourselves has promised to be with us, and to give us the strength necessary for this one day.

My final over-stuffed file would be titled "social concerns" if I had one. When I began this section on preaching I said that I had five bulging files, including one marked, "social concerns." Truth is I don't have a single file with that label on it. What I do have, all scattered around in those boxes of files, are sermons that I preached on the subject of society's issues – which is what we Methodists mean by the term, social concerns – and had all of them been contained in one file, it would be full to overflowing. However, I chose not to toss them all into the same filing bin because they dealt with varying subjects.

Subjects like race. Beginning my ministry on Capitol Hill, which was increasingly becoming a predominantly Black neighborhood, I could not avoid this issue. The whites that could afford to move out to the expanding suburbs were doing so in rapidly increasing numbers. The ones who had to stay put – or chose to stay put – felt abandoned and threatened. And, of course, they blamed the intruders who weren't satisfied to stay in "their place." Sad to say there were a few people – educated and respectable people – who hadn't even matured to the point of calling them "colored." So I dredged up a little song that we sang even in the segregated churches that I had grown up in:

> "Jesus loves the little children,
>
> All the children of the world.
>
> Red and yellow, black and white,
>
> They are precious in his sight.
>
> Jesus loves the little children of the world."

In one of those race relations sermons, I told a story about the day Wave and I were shopping for some furniture in a District of Columbia department store, and we spotted Vicky, who was three at the time, sitting with a little black girl in one of the over-stuffed chairs and sharing her candy. When I would tell that story I would usually follow it with those lines from South Pacific, "you have to be taught to hate. You have to be carefully taught."

Race followed me all the way through my ministry. Vicky and Tommy began their educations in segregated schools. When we moved to Bowie, in suburban Washington, Blacks could not buy new homes in that Leavitt development. Maryland, in 1967, had no open accommodation laws. I preached one sermon that I titled, "Think Black." "Just put yourself in their place," I said. "How would you feel?" Then I quoted Countee Cullen's heart tugging poem:

"Once riding in old Baltimore,

Head filled and heart filled with glee,

I saw a Baltimorean

Keep looking straight at me.

"Now I was young and very small,

And he was no whit bigger,

And so I smiled, but he stuck out

His tongue and called me Nigger.

"I saw the whole of Baltimore

From May until December,

But of all the things that happened there,

That's all I can remember."

Dr. Martin Luther King, Jr., was not seen as a respected justice advocate by more than just a few of my Bowie congregation. One prominent member of the church held a position high in the FBI's chain of command. Actually, he worked in J. Edgar Hoover's office. One Sunday afternoon, riding home together after attending a Washington Redskins football game, quite out of the blue, he asked if I had ever wondered why "the Director" referred to King as a notorious liar. I said that I had presumed it had something to do with King's alleged communist connections. "No," he said, "that isn't it. Tom, what I am about to tell you is top secret stuff. If you ever say I told you this, I will deny it." He then told me that King was a womanizer; even told me the name of his favorite mistress. Thinking that I had been granted some special privilege, I never even told Wave. Years later, of course, I read that the FBI was peddling this information all across the country, hoping to get the word out and destroy King's influence.

It wasn't long after that King went to Memphis and his death. It was a Thursday evening when I heard the news. I was in the church office finishing up the outline for my Palm Sunday sermon. The choir was practicing in the sanctuary and I went in to tell them what I had just heard. Friday morning, I knew that the Palm Sunday sermon I had outlined, ready to write, would have to be scrapped. Knowing the depth of negative feeling that some of the congregation had towards Dr. King – especially the FBI agent who had shared the skinny with me just weeks before, and would be sitting down in front of me, on the second row, his usual spot – how could I extol what I perceived to be Dr. King's virtues on this special holy day, and not have it look like I was shoving the savior of the world aside out of deference to one that I perceived to be a savior of our society. Here's how I opened that sermon.

> "On November 22, 1963, a forty-two year old man was gunned down on the streets of Dallas, Texas. I scrapped the sermon I had already written because I felt that my congregation would expect me to have something to say about that tragedy. On April 8, 1968, a thirty-nine year old man was gunned down on the streets of Memphis, Tennessee. I scrapped the sermon I had already written because I felt that my congregation would expect me to have something to say about that tragedy."

Race was never an issue that I could put aside. Segregation morphed into busing and that into housing and hiring practices. To the end of my preaching days, ever and again I had to address the issue of racism.

War and Peace is another of my social issues files. In the early sixties in northern Maryland some of the students Wave had taught started marching off to war. These were Maryland's equivalents to the Texas men that President Bush leaped over. Just as it was in the Lone Star state, the Maryland boys who had connections made it into the National Guard. When some of their families started receiving those dreaded messages that begin with the words, "We regret to inform you," I discovered an Old Testament battle story that is related in the second book of Samuel. The text I used for the sermon was this matter of fact statement from the second chapter: "There lacked of David's servants nineteen men and Asahel." "Nineteen men and Asahel" was the theme that ran through that sermon of mine on the consequences of war. A lot of numbers were coming out of the Pentagon then – how many men were missing or killed – and I wanted to remind the ones who sat out in front of me that morning that these numbers had names. Actually, it was when all the Asahels across the country started to be named that the legitimacy of that horrendous war began to be questioned more broadly. War, like race, was a sermon topic that never became uncalled for during all my years in the pulpit.

My social issues sermons ran the gamut. When the military was tied in knots over the homosexuality question, I preached, "Be Christian, Soldiers." One Labor Day weekend I took the parable Jesus told of the master of the house who paid all his vineyard workers the same wage, whether they had worked all day or just a few hours, and preached a sermon suggesting that a guaranteed annual income might not be a bad idea. This was a few years before George McGovern went public with this proposal, and even before Richard Nixon began to suggest that doing this just might be a constructive way to fulfill this country's constitutional mandate to "promote the general welfare" of all its citizens.

It is fair to say that I was never seen as a "radical" preacher. Some of my left wing friends thought I hedged my bets a bit, on some of what have come to be called the wedge issues. Truth is, I could never take off my preaching robe and put on my prophetic mantle. I always had to wear them both at the same time. Truth is also, however much I tried not to make my words out to be God's words, or lay any claim to knowing what the absolute right or the absolute wrong position on any moral issue was, there were times when I spoke what I honestly perceived to be God's will on such basic issues as love for neighbor, whatever that neighbor's color or sexual preference happened to be, and loving even one's enemies, and people separated themselves from the churches where I was the pastor.

What is true, too, is that in the later years, even though, on occasion, I would wrap the prophet's mantle around me as I took my place behind the "sacred desk", as it used to be called, I spent more of those fifteen to twenty minute offerings of mine dealing with care of the soul issues.

Which is, I think, a good way to wrap up this section on preaching. One day during my district superintendent years, Josh Hutchins, one of my favorite colleagues, who died at an all too early age, read a piece for devotions, written by a minister named Harold W. Ruopp. It's called "One Man's Journey." In that short piece, Reverend Ruopp is looking back over his ministry of thirty-two years, and reflecting on the three stages that he sees in it. In the first stage, he said, he stood outside the life process, "a spectator of a passing show". He likened it to sitting on the bank of a river preaching "sermons of comfort and courage to the swimmers who were in it." He would tell them which way the current was flowing, and offer them tips as to what to do when the going got rough. In the second stage, Dr. Ruopp said, he became the great helper, and from time to time would jump into the river, attempt to rescue someone and then hop back up on the river bank and wait for someone else to start to go under. "Then several years ago," he wrote, "because of circumstances beyond my control, came the third stage. Now I am in the river all the time. I am not always trying to hold someone else up; instead, I gladly permit another person to hold me up. I ask others to tell me which way the current flows and where the ocean is. I am no longer the savior; now I am the one who needs saving." Then comes the fourth stage, when all of us swimming along together, holding each other up, "shall learn to trust the river and the ocean into which it finally flows, confident that the river and the ocean and all the swimmers in it belong to God."

When I took the copy of this that Josh gave me, and stuck it in my pocket, I knew it was something I wanted to keep. At the time, however, still sloshing my way through a hangover filled existence, I didn't comprehend the truth of it. Now I do, thank God. Dr. Ruopp began by suggesting that this may or may not be the autobiography of other preachers. I don't know about others. It is mine, especially the autobiography of my preaching life.

Chapter 12

"Read, mark, learn, and inwardly digest."
Book of Common Prayer

There was another time when my life – at least my preaching life – passed before my eyes. It was an experience similar to the one I had when I was putting my sermons into more secure file boxes. This time it occurred as I was sorting through my library trying to decide which books to keep and which to toss.

When I retired, I decided to hang onto all of my books. Perhaps it was a way for me to resist the idea that my decision to call it quits really did mean that my ministerial career was over. Whatever the reason, I loaded them all up and toted them to our vacation home in West Virginia. There Wave and I converted one of the bedrooms into a study of sorts and lined two of the room's walls with my books.

Making the decision to put the house on the market a few years back meant closing down my study and letting the house have the three bedrooms the builders intended it to have. So one weekend, I took some empty boxes out to our house in the woods and began to take my books off the shelves, one by one.

Other events have caused me to sit up and take notice of the passing of time. Our children leaving for college caused a blip or two on my emotional radar. In a previous chapter, I wrote about the troubles I had navigating my passage through my decade marking birthdays. And much to my surprise, my baby brother turning sixty affected me much more than my own sixtieth birthday. In that same previous chapter, I wrote that it was my mother's death in 1975, 17 years after my father died that propelled me into my second round of therapy.

Packing up my books turned out to be another such rite of passage. When I climbed the stepladder to reach the books on the highest shelves, it suddenly hit me: this is it. I really am closing up shop. At some level, I already was aware of that fact. Pension checks had been getting deposited the first of each month for the past four years. But taking down each book – some of which went back to my seminary days – and deciding whether to keep it by my side for the rest of my life – there was a finality to this that I had never felt before. And sitting on the top of that ladder, I found myself mourning the death of a career – a way of life even – that had been part of me for almost 40 years.

I was also surprised to find myself reflecting on the various stages of that life – not unlike the stages that I would eventually note while leafing through my old sermons. Picking up a well-worn copy of Leslie Weatherhead's, <u>When the Lamp Flickers</u>, a book I told about in a previous chapter, I remembered those days when I was trying to decide whether I should leave the conservative church that had nurtured me in the faith. Reading this book was the first time in my life that I had seen, in print, questions that had been rumbling around in my head for years: Is there a flaming hell? Is every word in the Bible true? As I told you previously, this book, probably more so than any other, made me realize that I needed to move to a church that was more liberal in its thinking. So I put it into my "to keep" stack. Then there were the theology books that were so much a part of my early years. I kept all of my Reinhold Niebuhr books and one each from Tillich, Barth and Brunner – all theologians who helped shape my thinking in my seminary days.

There were lots of sermon books for me to weed through. I attended seminary in an era when ministerial students were expected to read the pulpit masters. Poets read other poets and novelists read other novelists, I was taught; so, preachers need to read other preachers. Preaching is an art form, my homiletics professors said, so study the styles of the best. I couldn't bring myself to part with any of my Harry Emerson Fosdick sermon collections, so well structured, so clearly written, nor, for that matter, any of the J. Wallace Hamilton or Frederick W. Robertson sermon books that I had. All these spoke to real life issues such as faith, doubt, spiritual uncertainties and social compassion, and they went into my "to keep" pile.

There were many books representing the stages I had gone through: the therapy stage, during which I read widely in the area of psychotherapy; my church-growth stage, when I was trying to figure out how to keep the numbers in my congregation on the upward swing. And there were more than a few books on death and dying, bought, for the most part, during that year when I lost my mother, a sister, and two brothers-in-law.

There were any number of "fad" books from the late 1950s and early '60s: books that fretted about having a Roman Catholic in the White House, others on the "Death of God Controversy." These were easy to discard. There was a shelf or two of titles on black theology and feminist theology, some of which I kept. It probably was a "fad" book, too, but I just had to put Bishop John Robinson's <u>Honest to God</u> – a frank, open critique of the Christian faith – with the other books that are going to travel along with me the rest of the way.

Handling all these books showed me where I ended up in my reading: devotional literature, for the most part. Care of the soul – my own – became my primary concern toward the end of my career life, as I began to reflect on what I had done and the meaning of it all. Thomas More's, <u>Care of the Soul</u>, which had helped me appreciate the dips and valleys and dark nights of my own life, was labeled a keeper. As were all of Frederick Buechner's non-fiction, and two or three of Thomas Merton's and Henri Nouwen's books.

It pained me to pack a large part of my life off to Goodwill. Many of those books had been with me for a very long time. They were like old friends, sitting there on those shelves through all those years, watching me – cheering me on, even – as I sat at my desk, under their watchful eye, struggling to do, as my bishop had ordered me to do, "take thou authority to preach the Word." But there is a time to keep and a time to let go, I told myself, and it was time, I thought, to let go of most of these old friends of mine. Vicky, my preacher daughter, had been building her own library, filling her shelves with books that reflect her new day and her own needs. A part of me, however, hopes that maybe, just maybe, she will want to carry along with her on her own ministerial journey some of the books that I could not bring myself to leave behind.

Chapter 13

"Sing them over again to me, wonderful words of life."
P. P. Bliss

In a sense I have been singing my way along this faith journey. I was born into a singing family. Although I am told Daddy sang in the Cumberland Presbyterian Church choir in Tennessee, it's Mama I first remember as the singer. She was also the one who played the piano for Luther and me as we made our debut as boy singers over station WDEL in Wilmington, Delaware. Our sister Elizabeth became our accompanist when we moved to southern Delaware and sang in church services there. Our first repertoire was not extensive, consisting of just two numbers.

"When through the valley, I'm walking down here,

When through deep trials I go,

Jesus, my friend, I will find ever near,

He will go with me I know."

The crowd favorite, however, was the more rollicking one of the two.

> "If you're in the battle for the Lord and right,
>
> Keep on the firing line.
>
> If you win the battle, surely you must fight,
>
> Keep on the firing line.
>
> There are many dangers that we all must face,
>
> If we die a' fighting it is no disgrace,
>
> A coward in the service he will find no place,
>
> So just keep on the firing line."

There was always a piano in the living room at home, and we did, as many other families did in those pre-television days, gather around it in the evening and sing. Usually hymns. In fairness to television, our favorite radio programs did dictate when, and for how long, we sang. In addition to our home singing, we sang hymns at Sunday school, Sunday morning worship, young peoples' society, and evening worship. We also sang hymns at the Wednesday night prayer meeting. When we got older, Luther and I joined our sisters and sang publicly as the Starnes Family Singers. Our signature number was Daddy's favorite, "Victory In Jesus."

> "I heard an old, old story, how a Savior came from glory,
>
> How he gave his life on Calvary,
>
> To save a wretch like me.
>
> I heard about his groaning, of his precious blood atoning,
>
> And some sweet day I'll sing up there the song of victory."

Then I went to a Nazarene college, where in multiple Sunday services and prayer meeting, we sang the hymns of my growing up years. Consequently, rummaging around in my head, along with lines of poetry learned in literature classes and dirty limericks learned in locker rooms, are hymns that, unlike anything else, including verses of scripture, have over the years brought comfort to my sometime troubled soul.

Do all these verses in my head and heart comport with the faith that I have come to affirm, however hesitantly? No. Take for instance a hymn that for some strange reason will make me choke up. As a matter of fact just before I wrote this line I was looking in a falling apart Nazarene hymnal that I have lovingly treasured, to see if the hymn I just quoted, "Victory in Jesus." was there. It wasn't, but in looking for it, I spotted, "Jesus Paid It All," and as I began to sing in my head,

> "I hear the Savior say, 'thy strength indeed is small,
>
> Child of weakness, watch and pray,
>
> Find in me thine all in all.'"

I got that same warm feeling – a teary feeling even – that envelops me every time I sing this hymn or hear it being sung. There is no place in my personal credo for any substitutionary theory of the atonement that this hymn implies. This theory, still widely held – witness the popularity of Mel Gibson's movie, "The Passion of Christ" – says that Jesus' death on the cross was a sacrifice made, on his part, for our sins. He was "the lamb slain for sinners" or as Isaiah put it, "he was bruised for our iniquities." I do not believe that Jesus death on the cross was anything more than an execution ordered by an oppressive political regime intent on keeping the masses under toe. Why then am I moved by a hymn that talks about Jesus paying it all? I'm not sure. Nor do I know for sure why I am moved by other hymns like it whose theology I have long since left behind.

If on one of those nights that I am channel surfing, I come across Billy Graham, mid-sermon, I will hear him out – however much I might disagree with the particular points he is trying to make – just so I can hear his choir sing that "invitation" hymn, "Just As I Am", that closed out so many Sunday evening evangelistic services that I sat through in those long ago Nazarene years of mine. On extended road trips, tired of National Public Radio, and thinking Wave has drifted off to sleep, I will sometimes scan for a so-called "family" radio station, in hopes of hearing a few of my old favorites. If Wave happens to awaken to the strains of some lyric that might mock the faith that both of us have grown to affirm, she no longer plays the scold – as she used to do – and question how on earth I could listen to such drivel. She has come to accept my explanation, that these old songs, for whatever reason, feed my soul.

Wave and I were having lunch recently with my college and seminary friend, Joe Williamson, and his wife, Donna. Joe's aunt had conducted the A Cappella choir at Eastern Nazarene College when he and I were students, and for some reason her name came up in the conversation. I said, "Joe, you'll never guess the hymn I heard last night on our local 'family' radio station. When I drove into the garage, the hymn just started, and I sat in the car until it was finished. It was the song that we sang every night on the A Cappella Choir tour. It's the one that your Aunt Esther sang a solo on the second verse." And I started to sing softly,

> "A wonderful Savior is Jesus my Lord,"

And Joe joined me in finishing that verse,

> "A wonderful Savior to me,
>
> He hideth my soul in the cleft of the rock,
>
> Where rivers of pleasure I see.

> "He hideth my soul in the cleft of the rock,
>
> That shadows a dry, thirsty land;
>
> He hideth my life in the depths of his love,
>
> And covers me there with his hand."

"Then," I said to Joe, "the choir would modulate down a couple keys, and your aunt would turn around and sing the second verse, as we hummed along behind her." And when I started to sing the second verse, so did Joe.

> "A wonderful Savior is Jesus my Lord,
>
> He taketh my burden away,
>
> He holdeth me up, and I shall not be moved,
>
> He giveth me strength as my day."

Alzheimer's is slowly taking away Joe's ability to recall the past that he and I shared and also walked away from. It is difficult for him to finish stories that he starts. He doesn't even remember a post-graduate year that he and I spent at Eastern Nazarene College, nor, for that matter, that he was elected to "Who's Who in American Colleges and Universities." All I need to do, though, is start singing one of those old songs that were so much a part of our faith heritage, and he has total recall.

Just last week I attended a memorial service for my Social Ethics professor from Wesley Seminary. He moved to the eastern shore when he retired, and Epworth Methodist in Rehoboth Beach where Wave and I attend became his church home. Haskell Miller was converted while attending a Cumberland Presbyterian Church camp meeting in Tennessee. Feeling God's call to preach, he went to college and seminary, and eventually graduate school for his Ph. D. For most of his ministerial career, he taught in college and seminary. He was a social activist, marching with Martin Luther King in Selma, Alabama, and taking a dwindling urban parish in the District of Columbia to use as a lab school to instruct seminarians on urban ministry. Two professors spoke at his memorial service – reading from his books that included a book of poetry – what you would expect for a social action trailblazer.

But, one of the hymns we sang was straight out of my Nazarene days. I mean exactly that, simply because I have never heard it since those days I used to sing it in those out of the way houses of worship where I knelt to pray. Even on all my scanning of "family" radio stations through the years, I have never heard anyone singing it. So at the family gathering after the service, to which Wave and I had been invited because Wave had worked with Haskell's daughter, Helen, in a suburban Maryland school district, I asked Helen why that hymn had been chosen. She told me about a recent visit to see her parents at the Methodist retirement village that had been their home for the last few years. Her mother was in the Alzheimer's unit and her dad was confined to his room having suffered a stroke. On the day of Helen's visit he was in and out of consciousness, and during one of his "in" times, he asked her to sing that song about "higher ground." And before she could dredge it up from memory – if in fact she knew it – this 93 year old social action warhorse – some would call a radical – began to sing one of those numbers he must have sung back in those Cumberland Presbyterian camp meeting days. It was then his daughter decided that when we all gathered to ritually send him off to his home over there, it would be fitting to have us all stand and sing,

"I'm pressing on the upward way,

    New heights I'm gaining every day;

Still praying as I'm onward bound,

    'Lord, plant my feet on higher ground.'

"Lord, lift me up and let me stand,

    By faith on heaven's table-land,

A higher plane than I have found;

    Lord, plant my feet on higher ground."

I was listening to Weekend Edition on NPR recently, and Linda Wertheimer was interviewing the singing group, The Anonymous Four. The group is breaking up, after just having released its final album. This album, for the most part, is a collection of old hymns like those I have just been writing about. They talked a bit and sang a bit during the interview. Then Ms. Wertheimer requested that for their final number on the air, they might "sing the one that touches a lot of our hearts." And the Anonymous Four, with their highly trained voices, began to sing on National Public Radio, one of those old songs that I had heard sung so often by some not so highly trained voices, in those little out of the way corners that we Nazarenes were trying to brighten:

"Sweet hour of prayer, sweet hour of prayer,

    That calls me from a world of care,

And bids me at my Father's throne

    Make all my wants and wishes known;

> In seasons of distress and grief,
>
> My soul has often found relief,
>
> And oft escaped the tempter's snare,
>
> By thy return, sweet hour of prayer."

Do all of us who carry these songs around in our hearts take them as literal truth? I doubt it. I certainly do not. My first Methodist Bishop, G. Bromley Oxnam, a freethinking liberal, used to say that creeds should be sung, meaning, of course, that liberties can be taken with lyrics. Poetic license is what we call it. No one seriously believes that Tony Bennett actually left his heart in San Francisco. When I was very young, I stuttered. "W's" just wouldn't come out of my mouth. Although it's been a long time ago, I think my "T's" did not come "trippingly off my tongue", either. What I discovered, though, was when faced with a sentence containing one of my threatening letters, all I had to do was start to sing the sentence, and that was all the permission my tongue needed to do its work. Creeds still make me stutter, figuratively speaking, of course. But if you let me sing the words of our faith – even the words that my head rejects – my tongue doesn't get twisted.

For the most part, I don't really think that the words are what warm our hearts. Rather, it's the associations we make when we hear these songs – especially the melodies. For me at least, these songs – hymns mostly – go to the depths of my being, and call to mind the faith I was taught, and have, over all these years, so wanted to believe. While writing this chapter, our three children and their life partners feted us with a 50th anniversary celebration. Our son, Tom, put together an audio/visual presentation of Wave and my life together. Most of it was visual with background music. It opened with pictures of our grandparents and our parents. As these immediate ancestors of ours' images were shown, Tom had selected the hymn "Amazing Grace". Pictures of Wave came next, and the music we heard as we watched her go from infancy through high school was the hymn, "Morning Has Broken." The hymn Tom chose for me was "This Is My Father's World." It's a hymn I did not grow up singing. It was not in the Nazarene hymnal of my day. It was one I learned when I became a Methodist. Tom selected it for my segment because it is my favorite. It's my favorite because it is my hope and my trust. Although, we never sang it as a family, it was the faith of my family. I was taught that this was our heavenly father's world. Make no mistake about it. "Just look at all He has done for us," my Dad would say. And as I looked at those pictures of me Tom chose to show – starting with a scared little two year old standing out in front of a rental house in Tennessee, diaper drooping down, holding a cat in his arms, and ending with a self-assured looking teen-ager shooting baskets in the back yard of a brand-new house in Delaware – listening all the while to my favorite hymn,

> "This is my Father's world,
>
> And to my listening ear,
>
> All nature sings, and round me rings,
>
> The music of the spheres,
>
> This is my Father's world,
>
> Why should my heart be sad,
>
> The Lord is King, Let the heaven's ring,
>
> God reigns, let the earth be glad."

I felt as if my heart would burst. Do I know for sure that Maltie Babcock is speaking eternal truth through this poem he penned back in the latter part of the 19th century? Not really. But it's a faith as trust that has stood me in good stead for my three score and ten plus years.

Fred Craddock is my favorite contemporary preacher. I heard him tell this story in a sermon preached at a worship service at the Chautauqua Institute. He was teaching a preaching class at seminary, and one of his students shared this experience. She was calling on one of her church members in the local hospital, and a nurse, recognizing her, asked if she would come say a prayer for a young man dying of AIDS. The nurse said that the young man's minister had come to call, and, fearing infection, pushed open the patient's hospital room door with his foot, and, standing on the other side of the hall, shouted a prayer into the room. The preacher/student told the class that she went to the dying man's room, crawled up beside him on the bed, and, cradling him in her arms, stayed there until he died. A student asked, "How long were you there?" "An hour and a half," she answered. "What on earth did you do for an hour and a half," she was asked? "I sang him hymns."

As I was writing this, I thought of another hymn from those long ago years that I never sing, nor even hear anymore. A verse of it goes,

> "Down in the human heart, crushed by the tempter,
>
> Feelings lie buried that grace can restore,
>
> Touched by a loving heart, wakened by kindness,
>
> Chords that are broken will vibrate once more."

I am told that my friend, Joe Williamson's, total recall of old songs is not exceptional with Alzheimer's sufferers. It seems that our brains have their own little secure vault where music gets stored for safekeeping. It's been this safe deposit box of mine – filled with all those stored chords from years of singing – that have keep me, like my seminary professor, Haskell Miller, "pressing on the upward way."

Chapter 14

On that best portion of a good man's life,
His little, nameless, unremembered acts of kindness and of love"
William Wordsworth

For all these months that I have been trying to fit my faith journey into a few hundred pages, it's as if my brother, Benton, has been looking over my shoulder. No, I make no claim to seeing "dead people", nor do I believe that there is anyone – no matter how much money we might pay them – who can put us in touch with some loved one of ours who has crossed over to the other side. What I mean by bringing Benton's presence into this Sunday school writing room with me is that in any faith story of mine, Benton would have to be one of the characters. But I haven't known how or when to bring him into the story except as an occasional reference, something I have already done. Which in itself is a good way to begin.

You see, Benton, in our family's life, was this shadowy presence – off on the periphery, in his room – as the rest of the family went on about its business. Don't get me wrong. He was a constant care, mainly for my mother, but shared by all of us. For all of my boyhood, I gave him the "bottle" (our word for urinal since we used a milk bottle), the bedpan – even wiped him, and rubbed his back with alcohol in the evening. In my teen years, I washed him, genitals and all. There was no escaping his presence – someone had to stay at home with him at all times. I remember my mother telling me that after Benton died, it seemed so strange for Daddy and her to lock the door of the house when they were going out. But after he left the wheel chair at age fifteen and moved into the hospital bed that became his deathbed at age twenty-seven, he never was present at any family meal, or at any family gathering in the "living room" or any other room for that matter. It is painful for us – the surviving children – to look at pictures of the whole family. Benton is in none of them. There is one that was made by a professional photographer. All of us are there including the husbands of the older sisters – dressed to the nines – all of us except Benton, who at the time is lying in his hospital bed not twenty feet from the spot in the adjacent living room where we are all, as we used to say, "watching the birdie." When we Starnes' survivors broach the subject, as we do on occasion, the best explanation any of us can give for this terrible insensitivity is a cultural one: that seems to be the way families handled such things then, we tell ourselves. Many of my dreams about Benton have him off in some attic room not being fed. That is not the way it really was, but dreams have their own realities, and mine tell me that the cultural mores operative in those long ago southern Delaware years, at some level, might not have been mine.

Truth is I have dreamed a lot about Benton over the years. Truth is also that he is the only family member, other than my Dad, who has walked across any of my dream stages. I used to wonder why I never dreamed about my mother, until it occurred to me one day that since Mama was never the topic in any of my therapy sessions, it just could be that she and I had few issues to work through. This was certainly not the case with my father and me. It was years after his death, and years into therapy, that I finally laid to rest my recurring dream that his casket was open in the living room, and instead of him being in it, he was milling around in the crowd of mourners who had come to "pay their respects." Bob Kirsch loved to parse dreams. However, he was no help with a recurring dream of mine that featured a needle-less Christmas tree – still decorated – lights and all – sitting in the middle of a living room months after the holiday season had ended. I dreamed that silly thing for years. Then one night my dream-makers placed that needle barren tree in Benton's room. And I didn't need Bob Kirsch's help in interpreting it. In my growing up years, in the family that Grady Starnes ruled, New Year's Day was the day the Christmas tree came down. No "please, Daddy, can't it stay up a few more days," could ever cause him to veer away from this hard and fast rule of his. Mama, ever the "good-cop", my dream interpretive self imagined, would probably then say: "You know, boys, if that tree caught fire, how would we ever get poor Benton out of here." Whether Mama ever spoke those words, I have no way of knowing. All I do know is that I never dreamed about a needle-less Christmas tree again.

"Poor Benton" was a phrase not used that often by those of us who shared his life. But it was something we all felt. When Mama would sometimes cry on Sunday morning because she couldn't go to church, Daddy having decreed that the children needed to be in Sunday school, and he, being Sunday school superintendent, had a leadership responsibility to fulfill, one couldn't help but feel sorry for "poor Benton" who must have concluded that if he were not around, the family could all be together worshipping in God's house. We all must have felt sorry for "poor Benton" when we loaded our new Chevrolet up that July day in 1941, and headed back to Tennessee, the first time back for all of us, except Daddy and Luther who had made a quick trip back a few years before. Benton would love to have gone back. Tennessee was the last place he had been able to put one foot in front of the other, however haltingly. Florine, who was married, came and stayed with him while all six children along with Mama and Daddy took off on a two-week vacation.

That's the way it was for "poor Benton." Repeated trips were made to Tennessee, and repeatedly Benton stayed home. His home wasn't his castle. A room in his home was. Sometime in the late seventies I had a Benton dream. I was hurrying through National Airport in Washington, D. C. toward the gate where my flight was scheduled to depart. I rounded a corner and there was Benton, in his wheel chair, directly in front of me. I stopped running and stood looking at him, all the while thinking: here I go again, off on a trip and leaving Benton behind. And in my dream, sensing what I was thinking, Benton said, "It's okay."

I preached that story in a sermon on grace; the point of the sermon being that grace was too big a word to be put into words, and the best way to talk about grace was to tell stories about it. I suggested that that is what Jesus seemed to do – his favorite grace story, I believed, was his parable of the prodigal son. My grace story, I told the congregation, was this story of Benton sitting in front of me, in his wheel chair, telling me that it was okay. All those times I resented Mama's shouting out the side door of the house, calling me away from the ball game I was playing with my friends, "Thomas, Benton needs you," and I would run in and grudgingly cram the bottle down between his permanently bent knees. Benton understood, though, my dream told me, that I loved him, and he didn't resent my being able to walk and run, even if it meant leaving him behind. That's grace, I preached that morning.

If Benton had been able to walk, he might not have influenced me in the way that he did. Nine years my senior, situated halfway between Ruth and Jane, Starnes child number four, he and I would not have been the buddies that we became. Unlike my brother Luther, I cannot recall a single conversation with Benton. Luther tells me that after I went off to college, Benton would, on occasion, lecture him on appropriate dating behavior. Luther tells me about other discussions they had. I remember nothing like that. What I do remember are hours and hours spent in his room, sitting on the couch by his bed, listening to "Jack Armstrong" or "I Love a Mystery," and tossing a wad of socks through an oatmeal box tacked to the top of a doorframe, developing what became an exceptional basketball shooting eye. To this day, I root for the Notre Dame Football team, as I do for Army, even though I attend the Army/Navy game with avid Navy fans, all because of those fall Saturday afternoons when I would sit in Benton's room and listen to Bill Stern call the games. Notre Dame was always my team; Army was always Benton's. Benton was my first playmate. Luther was four years younger than I, so I had to wait for him to become my buddy. Benton would show me how to make little cars out of what we called pasteboard. Benton and I would zoom these little paper beauties around the table – parts glued together with a mixture of flour and water – all the while pretending that we were the Green Hornet and his faithful companion, Cato.

It could be that Benton's greatest influence on me has had nothing to do with faith. Perhaps it has had more to do with what has been called the "survivor's syndrome." Some people who survive a tragic incident – such as a plane crash – feel a sense of guilt at having dodged that particular bullet. Why were they spared and not the others? I have never consciously felt any guilt at having beaten the genetic odds, and like my brother Luther, lived into old age. What I have sometimes wondered, though, is whether or not my overachieving nature is in some way traceable to the severely limited life Benton was forced to live? I have always looked to my father as the source of my drive and ambition, and to my mother as the motivation for my reading and studying. What also is a possibility is that I have been driven by a need to live some of Benton's lost life for him. Bishop Fred Wertz, with whom I worked closely for four years, said he did just that after his older brother died quite suddenly. Maybe this same need has been pushing me along in life.

Whatever truth there may or may not be regarding this so-called "survivor syndrome", Benton did give me some valuable lessons on faith and trust. I have already mentioned what he taught me about suffering. No way could I ever believe, let alone preach, that suffering could be tracked back to the hand of God. What kind of God would do this to such a gentle, loving person, like my older brother? Neither could I believe, nor ever preach, that God could, if he were a mind to, reach down and straighten out those rigid limbs of his, or put life back into his atrophied muscles.

Our little church believed in healing as curing. One year during revival time our pastor decided, along with the revival preacher, to come to our house and test one of those healing passages of scripture that assures deliverance if only one's faith is sufficient. The one that motivated our pastor and the evangelist of the year called for the elders of the church to come and anoint with oil the one who was suffering, and if this were to be done, James assures us, "The prayer of the faith will save the sick, and the Lord will raise them up." Well, Brother Andrews came to our house, along with the evangelist and some other selected elders, and we all gathered around Benton's bed. Mama provided the oil from the pantry, and the pastors bombarded heaven with their supplications as they put the Pompeian Virgin Olive Oil on Benton's head. Then Daddy and another one of the elders put their hands under Benton's arm and lifted him off the bed. Benton dangled there between the two men, his lifeless bent legs just touching the floor, his fear of being dropped etched

Through Fear to Faith

on his face, all the while being admonished repeatedly to just believe the word and he would be healed. When it was evident that healing wasn't going to come to the Starnes' house on this particular day, Benton was placed back on his back, with his bent legs still sticking up beneath the spread on his bed, feeling, no doubt, that if only his faith were stronger, he would now be running out the side door to go toss a ball around with Thomas and Luther.

But he never lost his belief in the goodness of God. As his strength continued to ebb, and extended bouts of breathlessness became more frequent, he kept the faith. Bright as he was, maybe that allowed him, like it allowed a lot of the rest of us Starnes children, and Mama, and Daddy, to a certain degree, to see through some of the more sensational faith claims, and hold on to the basics: that God is a loving Father of children everywhere, and this divine love is always there, whether deserved or not.

Benton has been my template for the good life. Never did I hear a word of complaint about the hand he had been dealt. God knows he had every reason to feel victimized, but it was a role he never played. He took some of the worst life had to offer, and made the most of it. He made no demands on those around him, and seemed pleased to take as a gift whatever time we would take just to sit with him in his room. And he never lost faith in the God of the Bible that he taught himself to read about.

Benton died on May 17, 1952. I was finishing up my sophomore year in college, half way through final exams, and had just fallen asleep when the dean of men tugged at my toe telling me that my brother had died. I knew it wasn't Luther. Word from home had said Benton was failing. The muscles of his heart were giving out, and he was finding it more and more difficult to breathe. He died in the early evening, right after

Daddy got home from work. My father always felt that Benton waited to die until he got there. Daddy went into his room and asked him how he was doing. Benton said, "I've had a pretty rough day." Shortly after that he closed his eyes for good. My sister Ruth, thirteen months younger than Benton, was in his room with him when he took his final breath. She told me just last week that she was so glad she was there with him. She said it was so reassuring to see him just quietly slip away.

The trip home for the funeral was my first plane ride. No one told me that planes landing at National Airport in Washington, D. C. sometimes approach from the south over the Potomac River. Just having that bit of information might have lessened the panic I felt when I looked out the window as we were landing and saw only water beneath our wings. This being the first death in the family, it was unsettling to see the crepe hanging on the front door of our house as we drove in the driveway.

At some point Benton had said he would like to be taken back to Tennessee to be buried. That did not happen. The cost probably had something to do with it, but not entirely. Delaware was home, now, and neither Mama nor Daddy would want their eldest son – the one named after Daddy – to rest in peace that far from them. His other burial request was granted. Somewhere he had read that "crippled people" sometimes had to have their legs broken in order to fit them into their caskets. He said he would not like that to be done. So Mr. Windsor, owner of the Windsor Funeral Home, said that would pose no problem. He removed the padding from the lower end of Benton's casket, and Benton slept in death, as he had lived in life, with his knees bent.

Five members of my family have died, and only with Benton do I remember the clothes each of them wore when they were buried. Benton wore a navy blue robe, with a light blue trim around the lapels that matched the ascot around his neck. I do not remember who sang his favorite song, or how it came to be his favorite. My best guess is that he had listened to Billy Graham on the radio, and had heard Graham's soloist, George Beverly Shea, sing it.

> "I'd rather have Jesus than silver or gold,
>
> I'd rather be his than have riches untold;
>
> I'd rather have Jesus than houses or lands,
>
> I'd rather be led by his nail-pierced hand.
>
> "Than to be the king of a vast domain,
>
> And be held in sin's dread sway.
>
> I'd rather have Jesus than anything,
>
> This old world affords today."

Benton was buried in the Methodist Church cemetery in Bethel, just a couple hundred yards from the house that I loved, and still, on occasion, dream about. Bethel is a quaint village on the banks of Broad Creek, registered as an historical landmark because of the significant part it played in building the ships that plied the eastern coastal waterways of Delaware. Bethel is a biblical name, given to the spot where Jacob had his vision of the ladder reaching up to heaven, and it means, literally, "house of God." Whatever possessed the early town fathers to name this little eastern shore town, Bethel, I do not know. What I do know is that there is something so right for Benton to be experiencing eternal rest in a church cemetery, in a town called "house of God," next to his Mama and his Daddy.

Chapter 15

"In our end is our beginning; in our time infinity,
In our doubt there is believing, in our life, eternity.
In our death, a resurrection; at the last a victory,
Unrevealed until its season, something God alone can see."
                                    Natalie Sleeth

Back a few pages, I ended my therapy chapter telling of the death of my long time therapist, Bob Kirsch, and saying that since I had lived through another of those decade birthdays that previously had given me pause – without incident – perhaps Bob's lessons to me on death and dying had taken. Maybe I need to qualify that assessment somewhat.

Reaching the three score and ten one – the one the Bible says is all any of us should expect to reach – has caused me to at least, shall we say, sit up and take notice. Are these ancient words, attributed to the writer of the Psalms, at the root of the traces of disquiet that I feel, I ask myself? If I am near the end of this race we call life, just how close to the tape am I, I sometimes wonder? The obituary pages that I read, now on a daily basis, suggest that odds are the finish line isn't that far off for me. Some make it into their eighties. A few reach ninety. Most, though, get three or more years added on to the ones the Psalmist said we could expect, validating the recently announced life expectancy for us guys.

True, I have made some peace with this. For one thing, I have lived longer than I ever expected. No reason, really, for having concluded years ago that mine would not be a long life. It could be that my mother's hypochondria had some effect on me. For her, every chest pain was a coronary, and every dizzy spell a forerunner to a stroke. Although my neurosis never reached that level, it has come close enough to make me a not infrequent visitor to doctors' offices in my early and early middle years. In a death and dying course I took some years back, the instructor asked us to make a guess as to how old we would be when we died. My best guess was sixty-two. So, I take some comfort in having exceeded my own expectations.

But all of this death anxiety can't be laid at the feet of Mama. The church we all attended majored on the subject. A fear of death was the most often used arrow in the Nazarene Church's evangelical quiver. Most of the Sunday evening sermons, if not all of the ones I heard growing up, contained at least one story about a person who rejected the invitation to "come forward and give his heart to Jesus" and that very night had a car wreck and was "cast into a devil's hell." There were so many of these, but only one I remember. It seems that a man, the evangelist told us, said that he didn't believe in God, and more than that, he had a challenge to throw at this supposed deity. So the man turned his head heavenward, and shouted, "If there is a God, let him strike me dead." No sooner had he uttered the final word of that challenge than a gnat flew into his mouth and choked him to death. Death for me in my growing up years was something to be, not just feared, but also dreaded; simply because death in my little church was always linked with judgment. "It is appointed unto man once to die, and after that, the judgment." How often did I hear that verse thundered from the pulpit and being born guilty, as seems to be the case with me, judgment after death meant only one thing – eternal punishment.

It was sudden death in particular that became my fear of choice. Cancer would give one a chance to "make things right with God," as my church put it – a window of opportunity for one of those eleventh hour conversions. And in my little town, just about the time I was ready to enter my teens, two of my playmate's fathers checked out rather suddenly. Charles Lee Morris' father said he didn't feel well one minute and the next minute he was dead at age 52. After dinner, Ann Larrimore's father said his chest hurt. It must have been the navy beans they had just eaten at dinner, they all thought. But he died within the hour at the age of 39. So heart disease in my young mind meant sudden death. And in my church, as I heard it said so often, "sudden death meant sudden glory." At least it would be glory for those who were "right with God," a status that seemed never to be within my reach. Then a few years later, the doctor examining me for life insurance turned me down for coverage because of a heart murmur, and told me that my basketball playing days were over. The doctor was not our family physician. He was on the insurance company's list of examiners. His being an eye, ear, nose and throat specialist, made his diagnosis suspect, not only in our family doctor's eyes, but in my basketball coach's eyes as well. A requested second opinion was granted, no murmur was found, and I continued to lead a fully insured athletic life. However, by that time, helped along by a doctor who never examined anyone below the neck, a few untimely deaths of people I knew, and consistent hell fire preaching, I developed a cardiac neurosis that, in varying degrees, has been with me all my life.

However, it is not the threat to my well being that it used to be. A palpitation can occur ever and again and not have me scurrying off to the doctor. I have come to understand that there are chest pains and there are chest pains. So every muscle catch in my chest can come and go without me presenting myself to the triage nurse in the local emergency room. A part of this peacemaking of mine with my ticker is that over the years other body parts have demanded that I pay attention to them. One of my eyes developed a leakage behind the retina when I had just turned forty, and in recent years has returned. My eye physician ever so gently mentioned the possibility of macular degeneration and has given me the little grid familiar to all persons predisposed to this disease, and told me to check, on a regular basis, to see if any of the lines appear to be wavy. I am checked annually to see if there is any sign of the return of the squamous cell cancer cut off my nose a few years back. And three years ago I was diagnosed with Type II diabetes, and amazed myself in the way I took this bit of bad news. For one thing it didn't send me into a state of panic when I was told that the risk factor for me having a heart attack was the same as it was for someone who had already had one. I did everything I was told to do: diet and exercise. I lost forty pounds, was taken off the diabetic medication initially prescribed, and feel better than I have felt in a long time.

So it does seem that I have made my peace with death. But something else is at work here: if my name turned up on an obituary page, hardly anyone would conclude that mine was an untimely passing. And for good reason. I have already received my biblically allotted three score and ten. My life has been full. My children are grown and leading productive lives. And all of my grandchildren are old enough to remember me. So no one could reasonably conclude that there was anything "untimely" about my death.

No one except me. Pascal's quote again comes to mind about the heart having its reason, and my heart still wants more time here on earth.

More adult to adult time with my children. And seeing a grandchild's high school graduation – or college graduation even – would be nice, not to mention at least one grandchild wedding. I have always been one of the last ones to leave a party. As long as there is something going on that interests me, I want to hang around. And for me, right now, life is still full and interesting. I am not ready to leave this particular party just yet.

My day will come, though. I know that. I still don't want it to come suddenly, and this no doubt is traceable, at least in part, to those scary hell fire preaching days of my boyhood. Wave wants to slip off in the middle of some night, she says. That's not for me, I say. I want some time to wrap things up a bit; tie up some loose ends with family and friends. But most of all, if I am honest, I want some time to get myself prepared for what that grace resistant part of me still, after all these years, perceives as some grand inquisition where the Grand Inquisitor himself will decide whether or not my life merits his saying, "well done, thou good and faithful servant, enter now into the joys of thy Lord."

Which brings me to a crucial point for my faith: what comes after this? Is there anything on the other side of that "valley of the shadow of death" that most people's favorite psalm talks about? I have preached that there is. Every one of the hundreds of funeral services I have conducted began with these words: "I am the resurrection and the life. He that believes on me, even though he die, yet shall he live." And not one single Easter sermon in all my years of preaching has failed to at least mention that this special Sunday, when churches are full to overflowing with people dressed in their finest – many of whom haven't been there since last Easter – is, in large part, a celebration of life's triumph over death; and not just Jesus' life, but our lives as well. This beyond the grave hope is in the marrow of my bones. I grew up singing about

Through Fear to Faith

> "A land that is fairer than day,
>
> Which by faith we can see from afar."

We sang a lot in those days about heaven, and what a joy it would be when we all got there.

Truth is, however, I never preached a sermon on heaven until a few years before I retired. For me the faith I was raised on was entirely too literal when it talked about that far away land in some "sweet by and by." There would be streets of gold, I was told, and gates of pearl, as well as walls of jasper. And better than all that even, we would meet and greet old friends.

> "When we all get to heaven,
>
> What a day of rejoicing that will be.
>
> When we all see Jesus,
>
> We'll sing and shout the victory."

When I shucked off a lot of that Biblical literalism, what I had left to preach about this so-called "hereafter" was some rather amorphous notion of a spiritual existence that death cannot cancel out. So that is what I would mention, occasionally, in eulogies, at Easter, or on All Saints Sunday.

Until all Saints Day in 1987. That was a glorious time for me. I was nine months sober, still basking in what AA veterans refer to as the pink cloud. I was reveling in being able to stand up before my congregation without thinking, "If they only knew." Preaching was a joy. The epistle lesson for that Sunday was from the Book of Revelation, and it mentioned a "new heaven." It talked about a time when there would be no more pain, no more sorrow, and death would be a thing of the past. The sermon had my usual three points, one of which was that there has to be more – something beyond history; if there isn't, as one writer I quoted years ago, and have since forgotten who it was, said, "we are over-provided for in this life." I never looked at the sermon again until four years later when the bishop asked me to preach the memorial sermon at our annual conference session. Traditionally, in the Baltimore/Washington Conference, the final Sunday morning session is a memorial service honoring the clergy and lay members who have died during the previous year. My old "heaven" sermon came to mind. I do not like to use old sermons, simply because whenever I have done so, there has usually been a loss of spontaneity and freshness, but it did comfort me to know that it was there, just in case.

During the few months I had to mull over what I might say, someone recommended a book to me. Knowing my love for sports, especially baseball, my friend told me I should read Bart Giamatti's book, <u>Take Time for Paradise.</u> Bart Giamatti, a Renaissance scholar, left the presidency of Yale University to become president of the National Baseball League, and then was elected Commissioner of Major League Baseball. Five months into this dream job of his, he died suddenly of a heart attack. His little book is a series of essays centered on his "conviction that we can learn far more about the conditions and values of a society by contemplating how it chooses to play, to use its free time, to take its leisure, than by examining how it goes about its work." With time running out on me to at least get a workable idea for my conference sermon I am nearing the end of Bart Giamatti's book, when I begin to read:

> "If baseball is a Narrative, it is like others – a work of imagination whose deeper structures and patterns of repetition force a tale, oft-told, to fresh and hitherto-unforeseen meaning. But what is the nature of the tale oft-told that recommences with every pitch, with

every game, with every season? .... It is the story we have hinted at already, the story of going home after having left home, the story of how difficult it is to find the origins one so deeply needs to find... . Why is home plate not called fourth base? As far as I can tell, it has ever been thus.

And why not? Meditate upon the name. *Home* is an English word virtually impossible to translate into other tongues. No translation catches the associations, the mixture of memory and longing, the sense of security and autonomy and accessibility, the aroma of inclusiveness, of freedom from wariness, that cling to the word *home* and are absent from *house* or even *my house*. *Home* is a concept, not a place; ...

In baseball, the journey begins at home, negotiates the twists and turns at first, and often founders far out at the edges of the ordered world at rocky second – the farthest point from home.... .

And when it is given one to round third, a long journey seemingly over, the end in sight, then the hunger for home, the drive to rejoin one's earlier self and one's fellows, is a pressing, growing, screaming in the blood... ."

So I took the old sermon and gave it a new Giamatti inspired twist, a new title – "Heaven as Metaphor" – and it wrote itself. Heaven is a word, I preached, that we use to try and talk about – to picture even – this sense that most of us seem to have that we are made for more than this. "What a piece of work is man, how infinite in reason" is how Shakespeare, and after him the composers of "Hair", put it. Heaven is a word that tries to convey this sense of home – this place we all dream about – where there will be no more sorrow, nor any more pain, because all "those former things will have passed away." Both my Dad, unsophisticated and unlearned as he was, and my therapist, Bob Kirsch, sophisticated and learned as he was, were absolutely certain, as their days were dwindling in number, that they were "going home."

God, I hope this is true. I really want to take all this singing that I have done all my life about this "Beulah Land" that lies somewhere out there in some ":sweet by and by", seriously now that I am staring death in the face. I want to know for sure.

But I know I can't. Even if I were not the "Doubting Thomas" that at age four dear old Brother Boggs said I was, I still couldn't be certain about that "land that is fairer than day." Faith, as Paul told us, even on our best days, is always "the substance of things hoped for, the evidence of things not seen." A friend from a church I once served lost her battle with cancer recently. Her pastor was comforting her with some assurances about that better place to which she would soon be going. Nedra stopped him mid-sentence and asked him how he knew. She was a person of deep faith, and she fought her final battle with grace and dignity. And if there is such a better place, she will be there. But she was so right. None of us really knows for sure.

So I have come to believe that that is where it has to rest. I am near the end. I know that. My heart longs for more. And somewhere deep within me, I believe Emily Dickinson was on to something when she wrote,

> "I never saw a moor,
>
> I never saw the sea,
>
> Yet know I how the heather looks,
>
> And what a wave must be.

"I never spoke with God,

Nor visited in heaven,

Yet sure am I of the spot

As if a chart were given."

Chapter 16

"Bring it on in, Reverend, Bring it on in"

When I finished my first ever sermon preached to an African/American congregation, I was concerned about two things: the absence of any "amen" or "that's right" coming from the congregation as I was preaching, and, why, toward the end of my sermon, did the pastor, sitting behind me, start his Greek chorus chanting of "bring it on in, Reverend, bring it on in." At a later time, I expressed both of my concerns to an African/American clergy friend of mine. The absence of any verbal response from the congregation, my friend told me, was simply an act of courtesy on their part. Since no one shouted "amen" in the churches where I usually preached, they didn't want to throw me off message. The "bring it on in" admonition was the black church's way of telling the preacher to get real. In other words, make your point. What is it you are really trying to tell us?

So I want to try and "bring it on in" here in this final chapter. I owe it to Herb, my wife's partner on the first ever debate team at Eastern Nazarene College – the one that whipped Harvard – and my friend, who, after one year of seminary tossed aside, not only his call to ministry, but his faith as well. Herb wants to know what I have preached. There are others, like Herb, who were with me back then in those "holiness church" years, and have since, like Herb and me, left the denomination that early on nurtured us in the faith. Maybe some of them might like to know the developing faith that has kept me at it. And, it just could be that some of my friends from those days – especially those college and seminary days – who remained true to the Nazarene doctrine, and have remained my friends, might be interested in what this "backslidden" Nazarene, now Methodist, considers his faith bottom-line.

Mulling this chapter over, I couldn't avoid shifting into my sermon preparation mode. And whenever that happens, I think structure, and that usually means "points."

And the first point would be the one I made back at the beginning: people can change. I still preach that; even with more conviction. It used to be that my prime example was my father. His was the personal redemption story that I knew first hand. A lifetime has given me more.

You have heard my redemption story. Nothing instantaneous about it, like my Dad's, except for the early February day something, or Someone, moved me to phone that New Beginnings' number which led me to Alcoholics Anonymous, and my new life. Dr. Kirsch was also an evangelist of mine, and Dr. Finn before him. My growth and change has occurred over time, and it is still going on, with fits and starts along the way.

But I know of others. My present pastor has a marvelous story – more like my Dad's than mine. He preaches his story so my sharing a bit of it is no violation of his privacy. By his own admission his family was dysfunctional. Both parents were alcoholic. There was a lot of shouting and chaos in the home. I was deeply moved by one Sunday's sermon when he told how the bathroom in his home was his soundproof chamber, and how we would slip off there when the shouting got to be too much, close the door, and sit on the hard tile floor and play Jacks, for hours on end. As is usually the case in alcoholic homes, Jack began to drink at a very early age. The drinking increased during college and became mixed with other drugs. He opened up a business in Rehoboth Beach, Delaware, which, unlike his life, was quite successful. Finally, the day came to him, like it came to me, and to so many others, when he had had enough, and he ended up in an AA meeting at Epworth United Methodist Church in Rehoboth Beach. After a few meetings, he decided to come to the church on Sunday morning. "What the hell," as he tells it, "I was going there two three times a week anyway; why not go back on Sunday morning."

Something – Someone, he is convinced – began to work on him. He liked and respected the minister – revered him actually – and one Sunday morning, sitting about four pews back from the front, Jack heard God's call.

That was 1994 and now Jack is the pastor at that same Epworth Methodist Church that he staggered into and began a life of recovery. He graduated from seminary, *summa cum laude,* and was accepted into Catholic University's liturgical studies doctoral program. He is a gifted communicator – able to hold a congregation, just this side of spellbound, with his note-less delivery, razor sharp mind, self-deprecating humor, and an uncanny ability to plumb the depths of his own feelings, and share that, without having you feel that you have just witnessed a bit of emotional show and tell. I marvel at his theological and biblical understanding. He has a familiarity with scripture and history that I find absolutely amazing, when I realize that he took his first step on this particular path just ten years ago.

Chris is another of my case studies. My wife knows his story better since he showed up for her Disciple Bible study class one Monday evening last September. She loved him from the start. His was a new found faith. Forty-something with a blended family, wearing, like a lot of us, scars from the past, he plunged into those thirty-four weeks of intense study of the scriptures even as he entered more fully into the life of Epworth Church. And last Easter Sunday, he was baptized and confirmed and triumphantly carried the Christ candle in all three services. He now sings in the choir with me, and wears his faith on his sleeve, in the most appropriate way imaginable.

There have been others I have met along the way, who, like Jack and Chris, have been captured by a faith in God that altered the courses of their lives. There have been others, unlike Jack and Chris, who found their way quite apart from the church. These people, like me, had been hanging around church sanctuaries for a very long time. They could sing the songs of faith with the best of them, and, if necessary, point a more than respectable prayer in the direction of the Almighty. But their lives were a mess, and traditional ways of getting one's life squared away were not working. And like me, a therapist's couch became a "mourner's bench", of sorts, for these, and a church basement, smelling of tobacco and coffee, but also reeking with the love and acceptance of fellow sufferers, became their holy of holies.

When I preach about changed lives, I am not just talking about faith-in-God-altering change. All I have ever tried to communicate is that whatever destructive path we may be on, we do not have to stay on it. We can change. Life can be different. And for me, it's any port in a storm. I happen to think the port of church has a pretty good record when it comes to change and redemption. But so does the port of therapy, and the port filled with all those "friends of Bill" just waiting to wrap their arms around you as they share their "experience, strength and hope."

That's my first point in this basic faith sermon of mine: people can change.

My second point is that wherever we go, whatever corner we turn, God will be there. With, I also believe, the strength necessary to make it through just that one day, just that one hour, or maybe even, just that one moment.

It's been seventy years since Grandpa Brakefield came down to the Cowan, Tennessee railroad depot to see us off on our trip north to Delaware, to hand Mama and her brood that grocery bag containing, along with the bananas, the apples and the oranges, the scrap of paper on which he had scribbled these words from the Psalms: "I have been young and am now old; yet I have not seen the righteous forsaken nor their seed begging bread." It was my great-grandfather's way of telling us that all would be well; we could count on God being around even in far off places like Delaware.

It was that way for us, as I have already told you. And it has been that way for me, as I also have already told you. And it has been that way in many of the lives I have seen lived out in the congregations I have served. There were precious children who died before ever setting foot inside a school building. There were two brothers – their parents' only sons – who died within a month of each other: one murdered and the other the result of an automobile accident. There were young fathers – young mothers, too – here one moment and gone the next. I have seen families struggle trying to deal with the disease we have come to call "the long good-bye" one. I have seen families live through economic hardship, and the dissolution of their marriages. I have also seen courageous acceptance of life's inevitabilities, and, more often than not, a deepened trust that through it all, whatever the "it" is, God would be there with them.

I have to be careful with this article of faith of mine. As I write this, thousands are starving and being massacred in Sudan, the AIDS virus is running rampant in all parts of the world, and the land we call Holy is ablaze. Just where is God in all this?

Here, the best I can do is let others speak. People like Nelson Mandela. Imprisoned for so many years, yet never losing hope, and using that confinement as an inspirational weapon to lead his people out of bondage into freedom. Even in the hopeless cases – like mass hunger or genocide – some who have been there are still able to see God's presence. Elie Weisel was sent to the Auschwitz death camp at the age of fourteen. One day he, along with thousands of other inmates, was forced to witness the hanging of a little boy whose crime was nothing greater than "stealing" a piece of bread to ease his hunger. His small body was not heavy enough to bring a quick death when the trap door under him opened, so it took a while for him to die. As he hung there, his little legs twitching, Weisel muttered, "Where is God now?" To which the man standing next to him answered, "He's hanging there on that gallows with him." The psalmist said that even if we made our beds in hell, God would be there. And Paul said in my favorite chapter, Romans 8, that nothing – in life or beyond life – will ever be able to separate us from the love and the care of God.

So I have preached, and continue to preach, that God will always be with us – no matter and wherever.

My third point is that human beings – every last one of us – are inherently good. Whenever I have tried to make this point, there was usually someone who wanted to know if Adolf Hitler gets a free pass from me.

I have no answer for that, except that there are exceptions to any rule, I suppose, but if I have learned anything at all in my relatively long life, it is that I do not let exceptions make my cases. They are just there. However, in the world in which I have lived, most of the people who have walked through life along side me, or sat out there in front of me on all those Sunday mornings, have been good people.

Including that wonderfully kind man in one of my very early church assignments, well respected and loved leader in the congregation, with a lovely wife and children. But one Sunday after church, the other man counting the morning offering with him, saw something he couldn't believe: this pillar of the church, or so it seemed to all who knew him, was palming some of the cash and slipping it into his pocket. His long time friend and fellow money counter confronted him, and, yes, that's exactly what he was doing, and had been doing for some time. Evil, corrupt – never would I use such words about this man. He was an inherently good man, who, for whatever reason, did a very bad thing.

Sam Keen said in a place I no longer remember that the worst word about us is never the last word. There is something redeemable in all of us. I am much more at home with Matthew Fox's notion of "original blessing," than I am with either Paul's or Augustine's notion of "original sin." If the authors of the Genesis myth of creation are trying to tell us anything, they are trying to picture the inherent goodness of all of God's creation – including the likes of you and the likes of me. And – in my mind, at least, and I presume to think, in God's mind, also – the likes of Hitler, as well.

So, I have preached, and still preach, that each of us is, in the best sense of the word, "a piece of work," made in God's likeness, a "little less than the angels," yet "crowned with glory and honor."

My fourth preaching point has been that although I trust Browning's words – at least the beginning of them – that God's in his heaven, I leave the bard there. I do not believe that all is right with the world. I do believe in collective evil, or to put it Biblically, "powers and principalities" that take on a life of their own. Reinhold Niebuhr wrote about moral men existing in immoral societies. The best of us can get caught up in the worst of structures.

So I have preached against the segregated society into which I was born, and though it has been opened up in many places, parts of that divisive wall are still around. I have preached against war, and while still holding to its necessity, sometimes, am moving ever so much closer to believing that war is essentially insane, and there's no escaping the truth of Jesus' prediction that "all who live by the sword will perish by the sword." I have preached against our taking Jesus' comment about the poor always being with us as an admission of poverty's inevitability, therefore, an acceptance of it; and, even worse, assuming that there was really nothing anyone could do about it, and instead, insisted on us keeping that quote in context, used by Jesus to deal with that particular situation. And, God knows, there has always been some despised class for me to try and speak a word of love and compassion for, and, if not that, at least some basic justice. It used to be blacks and now it is homosexuals. Groups that society wants to scapegoat – making them bear the blame for whatever collectively ails us. Society will, I think, eventually stop using the phrase "homosexual life style" and accept the reality that not all of us are wired the same way. We are moving in that direction – swiftly, it seems to me, since the debatable issue now is gay marriage having already, or so it appears, become willing to grant legal status to gay unions. The kingdom hasn't come, however. As Paul said, we are dealing with principalities and powers – evil ones at that. I had an African/American custodian once who said, "There will always have to be a 'nigger'; someone for folks to look down on." I had a brother-in-law who used different words to say the same thing: "Thomas, if I'm not better than a nigger, who am I better than?" I don't know who the next society scapegoat will be. There will be one, though. That just seems to be how collective evil works.

Faith will be my final point – appropriate, it seems to me since this subject was hit upon in most of the sermons I churned out over the years. It took me awhile – as I have noted earlier – to see faith as more a matter of the heart than the head. AA was my primary tutor here. It was in those church basement rooms where I first heard the phrase "turning it over." I had been raised on its equivalent: "Cast all your cares on him, for he cares for you." But that lesson never took. It was only when I had exhausted all the efforts I knew anything about to stop my life from spinning out of control, that I learned to turn it all over to the care of the God of my understanding – and trust that this higher power that I had been weaned on, could lift this oppressive burden and set me free.

Faith as trust – finally, I heard this graceful word. It is still hard for me to, as we say in the program – actually as I heard for all those years in those little Nazarene churches that I frequented – "let go and let God." But, I am getting better at it. And I am comforted by something we also say in the program: "it's progress we are after; not perfection." Turning it over, trusting, as I do, in the God of my understanding, does not free me from any responsibility. There are some actions I have to take. Which is why we join hands after every AA meeting and pray Reinhold Niebuhr's serenity prayer: "God, grant me the serenity to accept the things I cannot change, the courage to change the things I can, and the wisdom to know the difference."

In my preaching days I worked hard at trying to find just the right hymn to follow the sermon. If I were preaching this final sermon of mine, I would now ask all of you to stand and join with me in singing all five verses of this wonderful old hymn written by John Greenleaf Whittier. I first heard it when I became a Methodist. I loved it then, but now, almost fifty years later, I love it even more.

"I know not what the future hath of marvel or surprise,

Assured alone that life and death God's mercy underlies.

"And if my heart and flesh are weak to bear an untried pain,

The bruised reed he will not break, but strengthen and sustain.

"And thou, O Lord, by whom are seen Thy creatures as they be,

Forgive me if too close I lean my human heart on thee.

"And so beside the silent sea I wait the muffled oar;

No harm from him can come to me on ocean or on shore.

"I know not where his islands lift their fronded palms in air;

I only know I cannot drift beyond his love and care."